Havana

Mercedita Cabañas
Orozco
Guanajay
Bahía Honda Cayajabos
ROSARIO
DEL Soroa Artemisa
Candelaria
San Cristóbal

of Batabanó

——— Central Highway

——— Northern Highway

·········· Other Paved Roads

0   5   10   15   20
Miles

Isle of Pines

barbara long

A Rebel in Cuba

A **Rebel** *in* **Cuba**

AN AMERICAN'S MEMOIR

BY

Neill Macaulay

CHICAGO

Quadrangle Books

1970

Library of Congress Catalog Card Number: 72-101072

This book is for Carly, Bobby, and Jimmy

A Rebel in Cuba

1 THE PICTURE ON THE FRONT PAGE of *La Prensa* showed nine dignitaries seated in front of a huge portrait of Fidel Castro. The accompanying story in the New York Spanish-language daily identified one of the nine as "Dr. Manuel Urrutia, President of the Republic of Cuba in Arms." Another was "the young North American Donald Soldini who valiantly joined the forces of Raúl Castro to fight for the liberty of Cuba." The occasion was a rally in Newark, New Jersey, to raise money for the 26 of July Revolutionary Movement. I bought a copy of *La Prensa* at a newsstand on Broadway and took the paper to my room at the Hotel Bryant. I read the account of the Newark meeting and noted that the master of ceremonies had been José Antonio Pérez. On the editorial page, Pérez's name was also signed to a letter that declared that no one could deny the right of all Cubans to participate in the struggle to free the fatherland, but that everyone should be on guard against those who for selfish ends would exploit the revolutionary yearning of the people. The address affixed to the letter was 2380 First Avenue, New York.

I decided to visit Señor Pérez. Before going I got out my Spanish-English dictionary and composed a note that could be left at his residence in case he wasn't in. I took

9

the subway downtown to 23rd Street and walked across to First Avenue. Pérez lived in a fairly new building in a low-income housing development. I found his name and apartment number of a mailbox and walked up several flights of stairs. The halls stank of urine. I rang the apartment doorbell several times but there was no answer. So I slipped the note under the door and returned to my hotel as dusk became night. It was August 19, 1958.

"Esteemed Señor Pérez," my note began. "I am an ex-first lieutenant of the Army of the United States. I have just been released from active service after a tour of duty in Korea. I have some weapons which I would like to donate to the noble cause of Dr. Fidel Castro Ruz. If you are interested, please contact me at room 703, Hotel Bryant, at Broadway and 54th Street. Telephone Circle 6-2100. I am at your orders. Neill Macaulay."

The phone rang at about eight o'clock the next morning. "*Aló. ¿Señor Pérez?*" I asked.

"Yes," came the reply in English. And then after a pause: "I am very interested in your letter. I would like to visit you and talk about the matter tonight." That was fine with me, and I told him I'd be in my room from seven o'clock on.

After talking with Pérez I left the hotel to buy a newspaper and get some breakfast. *La Prensa* had exciting news that morning: the headline of the lead story was "Castro Foretells a New Offensive." Speaking on shortwave radio from somewhere in Oriente province, "Free Territory of Cuba," Fidel promised to take the offensive *pronto* to liberate the rest of the island. He said he was "very satisfied" with the development of the guerrilla struggle in the provinces of Camagüey, Las Villas, and Pinar del Río. But it was in Oriente that the greatest *fidelista* victories had been won: here Castro claimed that his forces had "totally defeated" fourteen enemy battalions and "completely annihilated" one of them.

I turned to the editorial page, where I found a letter signed "Dr. Raúl Chibás," which informed all Cubans in New York that Fidel's rebels were officially represented in the city by the Exile Committee of the 26 of July Movement, with offices at 305 Amsterdam Avenue. The people at the office, Chibás said in the letter, were fully authorized to collect funds for the Movement and would insure that all donations were properly used for the liberation of Cuba. That afternoon I set out for the Movement's office.

305 Amsterdam Avenue turned out to be an old brownstone building under whose second-floor windows hung a huge black-and-red sign proclaiming "26 of July Movement, Militants and Sympathizers." I walked up to the second floor and knocked on the door. There was no answer. The door across the hall opened slightly and a woman's voice announced *No están*—"They are not in."

"At what hour will they be in?"

"I do not know," she replied, and closed the door.

After wandering around the neighborhood for a while I returned to the hotel to await Señor Pérez. He showed up a little after eight o'clock. José Antonio Pérez was in his late twenties. He was clean-shaven and neatly dressed in suit and tie. He arrived at my room accompanied by a fellow roughly my age—then twenty-three—who wore a sports shirt. His name was Ginés Gorrín. We exchanged pleasantries in English, and I offered my guests cigars from an assortment on the bureau. Ginés declined but Pérez selected a fifteen-cent Dutch Master.

The weapons, I told them, were a Thompson submachine gun and an M1-A1 carbine converted to full automatic. I had picked them up in Korea and they were now at my parents' home in Columbia, South Carolina. I would gladly give the guns to Fidel Castro on one condition—that I be allowed to accompany them to Cuba. The fact was, I said, that I wanted to join Fidel's army; besides the guns, I was offering them military expertise. I handed Pérez my Certificate of Active Service, which indicated that I had been an infantry officer for nearly two years prior to August 6, 1958. To prove that the certificate was mine, I showed my passport.

The trouble was, Pérez explained, that they were authorized to accept donations but not volunteers for the Rebel Army. It would be very difficult. I emphasized my determination to join Fidel and offered to stay in New York as long as necessary for them to investigate me. Pérez remained dubious, but Ginés said that he would look into the matter. In the meantime, I should drop by the Movement's office on Amsterdam Avenue, which was open every night after six. I agreed to be there the next night. Ginés said that at the office I should talk with Donald Soldini, the American who had recently returned from serving with the rebel forces in Cuba.

I showed up at the Movement headquarters at about seven the following night. The scene was agreeably chaotic. Clean-cut young men sat around on desks and chairs, engaging in animated conversation. Cardboard boxes were scattered on the floor overflowing with printed and mimeographed propaganda. Quaint turn-of-the-century engraved portraits of the Cuban independence heroes Martí and Maceo hung on one wall; leaning on its side against the opposite wall was the huge portrait of Fidel that had formed the backdrop at the Newark rally. A small man about twenty years old, with the faintest trace of a moustache and wearing a sports coat and a fedora, introduced himself as Don Soldini. He showed me around the office and presented me to his comrades. After leafing through some of the propaganda—appeals to congressmen, the State Department, and American public opinion—I left with Soldini to get a beer.

Soldini said he could tell that I was a guy just like him —a guy who liked a good fire-fight. The boys at the office were talkers, intellectuals, and they would probably run Cuba after the Revolution. Soldini said he didn't care; he didn't give a damn about politics. He wanted to be back at the front for the final drive, but as soon as the Revolution came to power he would get the hell out. Why wasn't he in Cuba now? I asked. He said he had a bullet in his shoulder and had come to New York to have it removed. But the wound had stopped bothering him and he had decided against an operation.

I bought Soldini another beer and he told me about the situation in Cuba. He had served not in the Sierra Maestra but in the Sierra Cristal, where Raúl Castro was in command. This second "front" in Oriente province had been opened in April 1958, shortly before Fidel called a nation-wide general strike. The general strike had failed miserably, just as two city uprisings the year before had collapsed, each within twenty-four hours. The urban underground was a shambles, but the guerrillas were safe and sound in the sierras. In May and June, while Fidel and three hundred veteran guerrillas were confronting Batista's offensive in the Sierra Maestra, Raúl, who was under little enemy pressure, was raising an even larger rebel force in the Sierra Cristal. But Raúl was reluctant to commit his troops to combat, and this clearly disgusted Soldini.

"All Raúl did is sit around on his ass and send patrols out after the *chivatos*. Chivatos are people who are for Batista; they give information to the army. Raúl's patrols would take these guys from their houses and bring them to Raúl's camp and Raúl would string 'em up. Once in a while Raúl would send a patrol out to attack a *cuartel* —that's an army post—and that's how I got this bullet in my shoulder.

"Raúl got pretty pissed off at me," Soldini continued. "I kept telling him that I wanted action. Finally he kicked me out of his camp and told me not to come back. That suits me. I'm going to join this new expedition that they're raising in Mexico—if I can get enough money out of the Movement to make it to Mexico City. I've been drawing unemployment compensation, but now that's run out. That's why I've been hanging around the Movement here —trying to get some money out of them so I can go to Mexico City. Ginés—he's the treasurer—says they don't have enough yet. So I've been going to all their meetings helping them raise money—even been making some speeches. In my Spanish! They get a kick out of it."

As I ordered another round of beer, Soldini took some newspaper clippings from his wallet. They were from *La*

Prensa and one had a picture of Soldini shaking hands with Judge Manuel Urrutia—the man whom Fidel had chosen to be President of Cuba after the overthrow of Batista. Another showed Soldini on a horse in the Sierra Cristal. When I admired the clippings, Soldini suggested that I buy two bus tickets to Mexico City and that we join the expedition together.

"How long will it be before the expedition leaves for Cuba?"

"Probably a couple of months. Those guys are pretty slow."

"That's too long."

"Yeah, but Mexico's a great town."

"I know, but I can't goof off that long. I tell you what: I'll buy you a ticket to Mexico City if you get some contacts in Havana that will get me into the Sierra."

"It's a long ride from here to Mexico City. I'll have to eat."

"I'll give you what I can."

Soldini thought for a minute and then said that he would see what he could do. We agreed to meet at the Movement office the following night.

There were two college-age Americans at the office when I arrived. Soldini introduced me to them and then took me aside.

"They wanted to join up," he said. "A lot of guys like that come up here. Especially in the summer. Some kids say that they want to join up but they've got to be back in the States in September when school starts. We brush 'em off. I got it all fixed up for you."

We walked over to a desk behind which Ginés and a boy named Miguel were sitting. Ginés said he was glad that I could pay Soldini's way to Mexico City since the Movement was at the moment hard-pressed for funds. More importantly, I now learned from Ginés that it had been decided that I would be an excellent man for the Rebel Army. My instructions were as follows: I should proceed to Havana as a tourist, take a room in a hotel, and inform Ginés by telegram of my location. The telegram should be sent to his home address in New York. I should then be prepared to wait ten days or two weeks before being contacted in Havana.

It was Miguel who reacted to the doubtful look on my face. He said that if there was no contact after two weeks, I should call a girl named Isabel. He gave me her number and explained that she was working for the underground and that he and she were good friends. They used to have great fun chasing around in Havana in Miguel's jalopy, which they called *Mahoma*, or Mohammed. If I would just mention Miguel and Mahoma to Isabel, she would do everything possible for me. Miguel seemed very nice and obviously sincere.

Now that I appeared somewhat less skeptical, Ginés proceeded to tell me that the Movement in Havana would probably assign me to Pinar del Río province, where they had just opened a new guerrilla front. Miguel added that if I ran into trouble in Pinar del Río, I could find refuge at a Baptist mission in the mountains, *Los Cedros de Líbano*. The mission was run by an American family, the Willeys, who sympathized with the Movement and who could put me in touch with the guerrillas.

"Okay," I said, "now let me see how much money I'll have to give to Soldini." I took out my check book and subtracted from the balance what I thought I'd need for transportation and expenses there for two weeks. $150 remained, and Soldini said that would be enough for his trip to Mexico. But I had only $30 in cash and Soldini didn't want to accept a check. It was Friday night and the banks were closed for the weekend, and he wanted to get on the road before Monday. The problem was solved by Soldini's agreeing to accompany me to South Carolina, which was only slightly off his route to Mexico, where I could give him cash. Between us we had enough ready money for two bus tickets to Columbia, South Carolina. On Saturday Soldini would collect some messages to deliver in Mexico and we would leave New York that night. Ginés and Miguel were pleased with the arrangement. I suspected that they were rather glad to be getting rid of Soldini.

The four of us talked for awhile about the struggle in Cuba. "It is all the worst kinds of war rolled into one," observed Ginés, "a jungle war, a mountain war, a guerrilla war, and a civil war." I suppressed a slight urge to ask him why he himself was not shouldering a weapon. He and Miguel were too pleasant, too well bred, to be confronted with such a boorish question. Nevertheless, a saying that my father attributed to his grandfather, a yeoman sergeant in the Confederate Army, crossed my mind: "It's a rich man's war and a poor man's fight." Still, I expected to find many middle-class youths like Ginés and Miguel fighting with the guerrillas in the hills of Pinar del Río. In this expectation, I was to be disappointed.

In New York, however, the ranks of the 26 of July Movement were filled with young Cubans whose families had sent them to the United States for their education after 1957, when Batista closed the University of Havana. In the Movement office the students manned the mimeograph machines, collected money, and mailed out propaganda. They worked under the supervision of political exiles like José Antonio Pérez—men of Fidel's generation who were Cuban university graduates, lawyers, and journalists. Meanwhile, Pérez (whom I didn't see again after the first night) and his colleagues composed manifestoes, met with the leaders of other exile groups, signed pacts, and—or so at least they thought—charted the course of post-Batista Cuba. They were passionate about the idea of political freedom. On almost all their literature appeared the slogan: *¡Libertad o Muerte!* Liberty or Death!

I asked Soldini how many Americans were with Fidel in Cuba. He said he didn't know of any at the present. Three boys had left their homes on the Guantánamo Naval Base and joined the rebels the year before, but they were no longer with Fidel. There was an American, a man named William Morgan, who was a guerrilla captain in the Sierra del Escambray, in Las Villas province. But Morgan didn't belong to Fidel's 26 of July Movement; he was with an outfit called the Second Front of the Escambray, which was financed by ex-President Prío, whom Batista had overthrown in 1952. There were also some 26 of July guerrillas in the Escambray Mountains, though not many. Most of the rebels there belonged to the Second Front or to another organization, the *Directorio Revolucionario*, which was largely made up of students from Havana.

Later I learned that most students in Cuba who were active in the struggle against Batista belonged to the Revolutionary Directorate rather than to the 26 of July Movement. They were brave young people who played a deadly game of sabotage and urban terrorism. Few, however, were attracted by life in the Sierras, and those who were usually went to the Escambray where they could be with their own kind. Older middle-class opponents of Batista belonged to an organization called Civic Resistance, or to smaller underground outfits. It was not uncommon for one individual to hold membership in more than one resistance group. These organizations were cooperating with Fidel on the basis of a pact, dictated by the latter, that was signed in July.

On the morning before we left for South Carolina, Soldini and I visited several Cuban homes where he collected names and addresses of people to look up in Mexico City. On the street, between visits, Soldini amused himself by complimenting passing women in what he took to be a winning Latin manner. By this time I had reason to fear the possible consequences of his conduct. In the subway the night before, he had almost gotten into a fight with a Puerto Rican twice his size for paying too much attention to the man's date. But Soldini was undaunted and continued to play his game, urging me to join in the fun.

"When you see a good-looking broad coming up the

sidewalk," he said, "what you do is just stop in your tracks and watch her come. Then you slowly turn around and watch her go. That really shakes 'em." He performed this stunt a couple of times while I walked on, pretending not to know him.

Later that day, while we were killing time waiting for the hour when an important contact would be home, we visited the Museum of Natural History. Admission was free and Soldini said he always got a kick out of the stuffed animals.

I enjoyed Soldini's talk during the long bus trip to South Carolina. He mentioned running guns to the guerrillas in Colombia. He told me about the time he was hitchhiking through Alabama and was picked up by a militant segregationist, one of "Ace" Carter's organizers. Soldini showed so much interest in the cause of white supremacy that the guy bought him a chicken dinner and rented him a room in a fancy motel; even now in Staten Island his parents were still receiving literature from the North Alabama Citizens' Council. He talked about going with a friend to the Syrian consulate in New York to enlist in the Syrian Army; they convinced the consul that living in New York had made them realize that they had but one purpose in life: to kill Jews. The consult became so enthusiastic that he took them out to dinner, got them an appointment with the Syrian ambassador, and bought them airline tickets to Washington. The Syrians were about to make a big propaganda play out of the thing, when they learned that Soldini and his buddy were then only fifteen years old.

I didn't know how much to believe of what Soldini said. Essentially he was a joker. To him all ideology was absurd and all crusaders were crackpots. This went for Fidel, the Zionists, the Communists, Lincoln Rockwell's American Nazis, and the White Citizens' Councils. Even money meant little to Soldini. He was the real thing: a true adventurer.

Soldini said that on his way from Cuba to New York the month before, he had stopped off in Miami. At the time a Cuban Navy frigate was making a goodwill visit to the city. On the night of the Fourth of July, he said, while a fireworks display was going on in Bayfront Park, he and a Cuban comrade began shooting at the warship with automatic pistols from a deserted wharf two blocks away. A number of sailors scrambled for battle stations and began raking the shore with searchlights. Soldini said he and his friend withdrew without being spotted.

It was Sunday afternoon when we pulled into Columbia. I telephoned my friend Charlie, who soon met us at the bus station with his car. Charlie drove us around to several gas stations and open-air markets where I cashed enough checks to get up Soldini's $150. Charlie, an ex-Marine, was interested in getting into the Cuban Revolution, but he didn't want to wait two weeks in Havana. I told him that I would try to get him in when I reached the "front," and would contact him if it could be arranged. Soldini promised to let him know if there were any openings in the expedition from Mexico. After we saw Soldini off on a bus to Texas, Charlie drove me to my parents' home. Two days later I said goodbye to my parents, informing them that I was off to make my fortune.

I arrived in Havana on "Q" Airlines' $10 flight from Key West. The twin-engined Convair landed at Columbia Field, which happened to be the main base for Batista's Air Force. At the adjacent military installation, Camp Columbia, an infantry division and an armored brigade were stationed; these units, plus an artillery regiment across town at La Cabaña Fortress and a couple of training regiments and seven Rural Guard regiments in the provinces, comprised the Cuban Army. I noticed a few B-25's and Air Force DC-3's parked on the Columbia runway, but other than that nothing to indicate that a war was going on. Havana seemed to have changed little in the two years since my last visit. The building boom was still underway and new skyscrapers were going up in the Vedado section. In the central district the most noticeable addition was the political advertising. Posters had been slapped on buildings, walls, lampposts, the backs of park benches; banners were strung across streets; slogans were painted on sidewalks, curbs, and on the *Malecón*, as the seawall is called. All this was supposed to demonstrate that government and opposition parties were actively soliciting votes for the forthcoming presidential election, which, having been postponed in May, was now rescheduled for November 3.

I checked in at the small Hotel Pulman, which was one block off the Prado, Havana's main drag, and then went to the telegraph office to wire Ginés Gorrín. The telegram was sent to "Gene S. Goreen" at the New York address I had been given. "Mr. Goreen" was informed of my new address, told that I was having a great time, and urged to come on down. Then the wait began.

I spent most of the next four days in the water at La Concha, on the Gulf of Mexico. Havana had only this one public beach. The rest of the suitable shoreline had been appropriated by private clubs, hotels, and wealthy individuals. There was no surf at La Concha, but the water was cool, relaxing, and conducive to thought. It was quiet there on the Gulf, whereas downtown Havana was a madhouse of honking horns, racing motors, squealing tires, shouting peddlers, and supercharged conversationalists. Although bus fare from downtown was minimal, there was an eighty cents admission charge at the beach. This relatively high admission charge effectively barred the lower classes from this "public beach."

No message awaited me when I returned from the beach. No one knocked on my door at night. On the fifth day I decided to call Isabel, the contact Miguel had given me in New York. Although I was not supposed to call her until after two weeks had passed, I was thoroughly bored with paddling around in insipid water, reading Cuba's censored press, and watching bad movies. Besides, it was now evident that my money would not last two weeks, unless I drastically reduced by standard of living. I telephoned Isabel that afternoon.

It was she who answered the phone. I was an American, a friend of Miguel, I explained in Spanish. She replied in perfect English, "Miguel who?", and seemed somewhat annoyed. But I pronounced the magic word "Mahoma" and she became quite friendly. We chatted for a few minutes and made a date for eight o'clock that night at El Carmelo restaurant in Vedado. She described the dress she would be wearing so that I would recognize her.

I walked the two miles from my hotel to El Carmelo, arriving a few minutes before the appointed hour. It was a first-class establishment. I took a table near the door and ordered a beer. Isabel arrived precisely at eight. She was an attractive, willowy brunette in her early twenties who wore glasses set in large mosaic-like frames. She had done graduate work at Harvard Business School and was herself very businesslike. I got right to the point.

The Movement in New York had sent me to Havana to await contact, but there was one thing that bothered me: I had wired New York that I was staying in the Hotel Pulman, but now I had learned that there were two hotels by that name in Havana. I was afraid the underground would look for me at the wrong hotel—the one I was not staying in was the larger and better known— and, not finding me there, would give up on me. Since Miguel had given me her number, I had called her.

After questioning me about my motives for joining the Revolution—it was a good cause, I said, and I had nothing better to do—Isabel said she would discuss my case with Marcos, the Movement's national coordinator, who was due in Havana in a day or two. In two days I was to call her again and ask her to go dancing; if she had anything to report, she would accept the invitation and we would once more meet at El Carmelo restaurant.

The next day I decided against going to the beach. About noon, as I was walking along the Prado toward my favorite Chinese lunch counter, I ran into Don, an old friend from my home town. Don and two younger fellows whom I didn't know were in Havana for a brief vacation. In hushed tones I explained that I was working for the Revolution. They were impressed.

Over lunch Don said that they had found a great whorehouse the night before and were planning to visit it again that afternoon. They invited me to go along and I did, although I told them that I wouldn't join in the fun, because, as a poor revolutionary, I couldn't afford it.

I didn't tell them the real reason for my abstinence: that I was recently married. My wife and I had eloped the week before I had contacted the Movement in New York. Since I had just gotten out of the army and had no means of supporting her and no place for us to live, we agreed that she would return to her parents and to school at the University of Michigan, while I would go on to Cuba and rise to power with the revolutionary forces. I guessed that the war would be over by the end of the semester and, by that time, I should have acquired a home and a livelihood. In the meantime, we decided to keep our marriage a secret.

The whorehouse I visited with Don and his friends bore a striking resemblance to the Arsenal Hill Teen Canteen in our home town. The walls of the main room were painted in cool pastels. It was furnished with spotless, linoleum-topped tables and chairs arranged around a small dance floor. There was a brightly bubbling jukebox with rock-and-roll records, and a bar. The girls, all teen-agers, were dressed in shorts and halters. All were white and several blonde, though their eyes were unmistakably Latin. It was a place where American high-school and college boys of the 1950's came to relieve their sexual tensions in surroundings that were not forbiddingly foreign.

We were the first to arrive that afternoon, and the madam zestfully announced *los americanitos* as she escorted us through the hall past the girls' room to the canteen. It was not long before we were joined by four lively *muchachas* who spoke passable English. As Don and his friends drifted off to the bedrooms with girls, I sipped my beer and tried to convince the remaining girl that, though I liked her, I couldn't take her to bed. Finally she excused herself and wandered away. I decided that Cuban whores were probably the most polite in the Western Hemisphere; any *gringo* who went to a Mexican bordello and refused its offerings would be sneered at, called a *cabrón* or a *maricón*, and, perhaps, spit upon.

That night I joined Don and his friends at the Tropicana, a huge open-air night club and gambling casino in the suburb of Marianao. They played roulette and blackjack, and I said to hell with my budget and got completely smashed on rum and Coke. I recall repeatedly swaggering up to the bar and announcing in Spanish: "What I want is a Cuba Libre." My compatriots departed for home the next morning leaving me with a monstrous hangover. I had had my fill of the pleasures of Havana; I wanted to get on with the Revolution. That night I met Isabel for the second time at El Carmelo.

Marcos had not arrived, but Isabel had talked with some other important members of the Movement and they wanted to send me to Pinar del Río as soon as possible to join the forces of Comandante Dirmidio Escalona. Yet I would still have to wait for Marcos' approval. Isabel and

I would meet again the next day at the corner of 23rd and G Streets. Down the center of G Street, also called Avenue of the Presidents, ran a palm-lined promenade, and there were numerous benches where couples sat and talked. On one of these benches I learned that Marcos was still out of town but that the Movement was going ahead with arrangements to send me to the "front." If all went well, Isabel and I would leave on the Monday afternoon train for Pinar del Río City. I was to telephone her at nine o'clock Monday morning for final confirmation.

At the appointed time I called and asked if everything was set for our excursion into the country. "No," she said, "it is not possible." Isabel seemed distraught, almost lapsing into Spanish. I asked to see her that day and she agreed to meet me at the same place.

When Isabel arrived, she was quite composed. She admitted that she was nervous talking to me on the phone; she had just found out that the police were bugging her line. Anyway, something had come up that made it necessary to postpone my departure for the hills. I did not ask her to explain. I was willing to wait till the right moment, I assured her, but added that I was almost broke; in another day I would have to stop eating. Isabel gave me five pesos and told me to meet her again tomorrow.

At our next meeting Isabel said that it had been arranged for me to move in with the family of a member of the Movement in Havana. I was to check out of my hotel the following day and come to that same corner, where Isabel's sister would meet me and take me to my new lodgings. I thanked her, and we said goodbye for the last time.

The girl who met me the next day bore little resemblance to her sister. She spoke no English; though I didn't know it at the time, it would be more than two months before I would have another opportunity to converse in my native language. We hailed a taxi and she directed the driver to a building in a mixed commercial-residential section not far from the center of the city. We climbed a flight of stairs to the modest apartment of a man called Manolo. Isabel's sister introduced me to my host and his wife, drank a cup of coffee with us, and left.

Manolo, an erstwhile waiter at the Hotel Nacional, was an invalid. In May 1957, while a labor organizer for the 26 of July Movement, he was accosted by the police. In attempting to run he was cut down by a burst of submachine gun fire. A bullet hit his spinal column, permanently paralyzing his legs. After two months and seven days in police custody, he was released. The *batistianos* thought they had rendered him harmless; who knows, perhaps they considered him a good living example to other workers who might be tempted to take the revolutionary path. But Manolo, in his wheel chair and in the seclusion of his second-floor apartment, continued to serve the Revolution. He was no ordinary man. He had a quick mind and an iron will. He was a decision-maker: a comandante of the 26 of July underground.

Manolo's lovely wife was a chambermaid at the Havana Hilton. They had one child: a handsome, well-disciplined, and quick-witted boy of eight. They shared the two-room apartment with Manolo's brother, a waiter at the Hilton. Another brother, who worked at the same hotel, usually dropped by after work and sometimes spent the night. This brother and I slept on the kitchen floor.

Manolo was no ideologue. He was a fidelista because he believed Fidel would improve the lot of the Cuban people. There was no Marxist jargon in his talk and he had some good words for the United States: "In your country the worker earns much money." He even admired the South: "There you have the correct attitude toward the Negroes." Politely I suggested that the Cuban policy of racial integration was better.

"No," he insisted, "your system is better. The Negroes here are pimps and *marijuaneros*. They flock to join Batista's army. *Los negros* are not revolutionaries. *Bueno*, among one thousand revolutionaries, there might be one Negro." He told me about a Negro with Escalona who was a splendid fellow. But most blacks, Manolo felt, were potential chivatos—informers. They abandoned their wives and children; how could you expect them to be loyal to the Revolution?

Apart from these views, I liked Manolo immensely. But I was not unhappy when on the morning of September 12 he announced that I would leave for the hills that night. At sundown a taxi driven by a member of the Movement parked at the curb below the apartment. Manolo told me to take along my spare clothes, which were all in one grip, and my passport. Should we be stopped on the road by batistianos I was to pose as an American engineer who had hired the taxi to take him to the copper mines at Matahambre. It would be all right to wear my walking boots, which I had had custom-made in Hong Kong earlier in the year for use in the Cuban Revolution. The driver would take me to the home of a revolutionary in the sugar-mill village of Mercedita. There I was to give my grip and my passport to the driver so he could bring them back to Havana where Manolo would keep them for me.

Before leaving I embraced Manolo and his family. The thought of their kindness and camaraderie nearly overwhelmed me. Later Manolo told me that if I had displayed any signs of untrustworthiness they would have killed me.

out of his back pocket a silvery object several times longer than the pistol.

"What I do not understand," he said as he sat down, placing the magazine in his lap, "is why you Americans support Batista."

"I do not support Batista any more than you do," I countered. "It is a thing of the government. President Eisenhower is *muy equivocado* in his policy toward Cuba, and toward Latin America in general."

"Some day you will have a revolution there in *los Estados Unidos*."

Our discussion ended with the arrival of Captain Claudio's mother. She was a strikingly handsome woman, who looked no more than forty years old. Many times in the months to come I would be reminded of the beauty and *dignidad* of revolutionary womanhood. Claudio's mother gave me a brown paper bag with a rebel uniform: cotton shirt and trousers dyed olive-green, and a red-and-black 26 of July armband. "You may put these on when you are in the hills," she said, and smiled, though her eyes were sad. I would not need shoes; everyone agreed that my Hong Kong boots were magnificent.

We left at 9:30 in the Toyota. I sat in the back; the man with the machine pistol was in the front next to the driver, his weapon at the ready. "If they stop us now," he remarked as we entered the narrow country road, "we will have to fight." There was no moon and we had to drive with lights on.

After about fifteen minutes we arrived at a cabin constructed of palm branches called a *bohío*. The place was deserted. "Go inside," the big man said. "You will have to wait here until midnight." At that time a peasant named

Juan would come for me. After the lights of the Toyota disappeared around a curve in the road to Mercedita, I lay down on a bed of burlap sacks stretched across a wooden frame, and waited.

At midnight I was roused from a light sleep by whispered cries of *¡Americano! ¡Americano!* It was Juan, my guide, a sturdy fellow of about thirty. He had only one horse, which he insisted that I mount. I protested, saying that I was perfectly capable of walking behind the animal. But Juan explained that since it was a dark night and our path would be rough, it was better for him to walk ahead leading the horse. Much of the route was along the grass-covered tracks of a sugar-mill railroad.

Just before dawn we arrived at the house of Titi in the foothills of the sierra. While Juan went inside to confer with Titi, I sat in the damp grass on the edge of the trail. We left the horse at the house and, as day began to break, Juan and I began our hike into the mountains. Titi was to join us later and guide us into the rebel camp.

The tropical sun rose over our backs like a great red ball. Soon it was lashing us with waves of white-hot humidity. We scurried along a grassy ridge. Below us on both sides a green mantle of sugar cane covered the lesser hills and flowed off into the lowlands. A warm breeze rustled the cane, wafting its sweetness to our nostrils. Ahead loomed a forest-covered mountain. When at last we entered the forest we came upon a brook, which we followed upstream for a few hundred yards. Then we sat down in a cool and pleasant clearing to wait for Titi.

Titi, a smiling, moustachioed country boy of about nineteen, appeared about an hour later, a sack filled with canned food slung over his shoulder. Like Juan, Titi wore the typical broad-brimmed straw hat of the peasant. This young man played a vital role in the revolutionary struggle in eastern Pinar del Río as Claudio's link with the revolutionaries in the lowlands. Whenever possible Titi, who lived with his parents in the house in the cane fields at the foot of the mountains, was informed of the whereabouts of the guerrillas. It was he who expedited the flow of supplies, messages, intelligence, and personnel between the lowlands and the sierra.

Juan relieved Titi of the sack and the three of us renewed our march up the trail by the brook. A few minutes later we halted and Titi made a bird call by sucking vigorously on the back of his hand. An answer in kind came from further up the path, and soon we were embracing two uniformed and bearded sentries. The rebel camp was on a slope where there were enough saplings under the canopy of larger trees for hanging the band's hammocks, which were strung up in no discernible pattern. Young men, some of them bearded, sat on the ground silently playing cards, cleaning weapons, listening to a transistor radio playing at low volume, or conversing in whispers. Manolo was wrong about only one revolutionary in a thousand being a Negro; among fewer than two dozen fidelistas in this camp, three were black and two were mulatto.

Captain Claudio's bushy black beard made him appear much older than his twenty-one years. His large brown eyes had long, almost feminine lashes; when he smiled, which was often, they twinkled and he looked a little like a dark Santa Claus. He was short and powerfully built and, like so many rural and small-town Cubans, disarmingly soft-spoken. Claudio exuded quiet confidence; he was, as I would learn, imperturbable and incredibly tough —both mentally and physically. There could be no question about his being the natural leader of this band.

Claudio had more formal education than any of the Cubans under his command. As the son of a foreman at the Mercedita sugar mill, he was able to finish high school and go on to the University of Havana where he studied sculpture at the School of Fine Arts. If he was devoted to art, he gave no strong indication of it other than listening with amused interest to my description of some works of Michelangelo that I had seen in Rome. He was curious about many things, but he was most concerned with immediate, practical matters. He believed in the Revolution, but he didn't seem to know why and he didn't care. Political philosophy held little value for him; on political matters, he trusted his instincts. He expressed mild contempt for exiled intellectuals like Mario Llerena—a native of Cabañas, the closest town to Mercedita—whom he referred to as *un bicho*. On occasions, when the censorship was lifted, the Cuban press published erudite articles by Llerena praising democracy and condemning dictatorship. Claudio's writing was confined to unpublishable letters and reports which were characterized by atrocious spelling; in even the most common words he would substitute a *v* for a *b*.

Claudio's education was cut short when Batista closed the university in 1957. Thereafter he devoted full time to revolutionary activity in the Cabañas-Mercedita area. After the general strike of April 1958, he and two companions—El Gallego, a stevedore, and Pipilo, a Negro sugar worker—disarmed a batistiano jeep patrol and took to the hills with an automatic carbine and two submachine guns. By the time I arrived on September 13, Claudio had built a band of seventeen guerrillas. All went by *noms de guerre*.

El Gallego, who was about forty and Claudio's second-in-command, was from the port of Mariel. Others were the sons of small sugar farmers, or mill workers of Mercedita or Cabañas. These included Pancho, a beardless white boy of nineteen; Tite, a handsome mulatto; and Changó, a black. Some were from Havana: El Habanero, a bus driver; Ramoncito, a gardener; Sosa, a mulatto hospital worker who became the band's medic; and Quintín, a little Negro laborer who was said to have killed twenty policemen. From various parts of Havana and Pinar del Río provinces came Mesa, Alberto, Cucalambé, and San Antonio. The last, whose *nom de guerre* derived from his home town, had a high school education and was the group's only practicing Catholic. El Indio, who had a trace of Chinese blood, was a barber; Mateo was an ex-soldier. Chicho was the only mountain peasant who regularly marched with Claudio in September. Tío, who was somewhat older than El Gallego, was a peasant who often cooked for the guerrillas when the band was in camp. Other peasants served as guides when the outfit was on the march. Claudio felt that the peasants of the sierra served the Revolution best by living at home, where they could gather vital intelligence and facilitate the shipment of food and other supplies to the guerrillas.

Besides Claudio's troops there were in the camp several men who, like me, were recruits for the group under the personal command of Comandante Escalona. One of these was César, whose father ran a cubbyhole drugstore in a working-class neighborhood in Havana. César, who was twenty-three years old and had studied accounting at the university, was to become Escalona's adjutant. Like Claudio, he had an easy manner that masked an iron will. He had belonged to the Revolutionary Directorate in Havana and had taken part in a number of student demonstrations—including one protesting a visit by Vice President Nixon. His background was unique among the guerrillas of Pinar del Río.

A city girl called Lila was also in the camp. She was short, on the plumpish side, and wore her long black hair in pigtails. Lila dressed in the rebel uniform and kept a small .22 caliber automatic at her belt. Her exposed skin was covered with mosquito bites. She had fallen in love with the chief of the 26 of July underground in Pinar del Río City and, until the capture of her lover, served the Movement as a courier between the provincial capital and Havana. He was tortured by the batistianos. When they released him he was a physical wreck—subject to violent headaches, attacks of amnesia, and epileptic-like fits. "They made him so he was no good as a man," Lila said. Continuing his revolutionary activities, he was apprehended for the second time in a police raid on Lila's Havana apartment. Unable to endure another session with Batista's torturers, he asked Lila to bring him some "headache" pills, which she knew to be cyanide. Lila watched her lover die at her dining-room table.

Lila had come to Claudio's camp from Havana with messages from the underground and a few cartridges. She would return to the capital about a week after my arrival.

Eventually she reached the Sierra Maestra, where she joined Fidel for the last weeks of the guerrilla struggle.

Claudio decided to break camp on the day that I arrived. They had been too long in one place, and he believed it prudent to shift around within an area of twenty or thirty square miles while awaiting Escalona. After an early supper of rice, black beans, and fried pork, we moved out. It was roughly an hour before sunset. My pack must have weighed forty pounds, and its straps were soon cutting painfully into my shoulders. I was glad that Claudio had issued me an M-1 carbine, a relatively light weapon. The others, I knew, bore heavier burdens—except for Lila, who rode a horse provided by one of the guides. It was almost night when we left the footpath along which we had been moving and entered a dirt road. There was no moon, but the stars provided enough light for travel.

We walked on that road for four hours. During the last two of those hours I was afraid that I would collapse at any moment. Rest periods were few and brief. The grades were so steep it seemed to me that no motor vehicle could conquer them. Finally, about midnight we veered off the road at its junction with a forest trail, where Claudio announced that we would camp until dawn. I crumpled to the ground where I stood, content to lie there, my head resting on my pack, until sunrise. Everyone else was stringing up hammocks. Claudio walked over to ask if I were not going to do likewise. My instinct was to reply negatively, but since I vaguely sensed that the image of the United States in that part of the underdeveloped world hung on my reply, somehow I mustered enough strength to stagger to my feet, extract my hammock, and tie it between two small trees. For the first time I regretted that I had spent my tour of duty in Korea as a Post Exchange officer instead of in the field conditioning myself for this adventure.

During the next few days I gradually got into shape. I would never be the equal of a Cuban peasant, but at least I would not hold the band back. Actually, Claudio's guerrillas had an easier time during the first two weeks that I was with them than in any period prior to December. In September we were never on the march for more than six hours at a time; and some days we did not move at all. We always had plenty of food. The men were in high spirits; there was even some horseplay. While Lila was with us Cucalambé specialized in cutting loud farts—of both real and simulated varieties—which she tried to ignore.

We had time to swim in rock-bound pools fed by mountain streams, and once I went with Claudio, Quintín, Pancho, and Pipilo to explore a cave. We carried only side arms. I didn't have a pistol at the time, but tied to my cartridge belt were two hand grenades which had been loaded and fused by the underground and were commonly called *piñas*, or pineapples. We entered the mouth of the cave and searched its interior with flashlights. We saw a small opening at the top of a steep incline. Since *el americano* was the largest of the bunch, all could get through the aperture if I could; with me in the lead we began to climb toward it. About halfway up a hand grenade got loose. As it began its bounding descent, in my excitement I confused the Spanish words for pineapple and penis. "¡*Cui-*

dado!" I shouted, with visions of us all being blown to hell. "*La pinga* is falling!" My comrades were immobilized with laughter. They hooted even louder when I finally got it across that I was talking about a live hand grenade. At length we recovered the runaway piña from among the rocks on the floor of the cave. There had been no danger: three weeks later when I removed the safety pins from both grenades and tossed them at the enemy, neither exploded.

Escalona joined forces with Claudio toward the end of September. The Comandante was twenty-nine years old and a native of Holguín in Oriente province. He was of average height for a Cuban and slenderly built. Among his troops, some three dozen wiry farmers and workers, he seemed almost delicate, but, as I was soon to learn, there was no man in the sierra with more endurance; he carried his own pack, and as his personal weapon he chose a foot soldier's M-1 rifle. He had an ample beard, a straight nose, and eyes that always seemed to be searching for something. When he smiled, it was only a half-smile. He was a man consumed by duty; Fidel had no more loyal lieutenant. At times he seemed devoid of all imagination, but he got the job done. He had caution in abundance. Although I sometimes got the impression that he was beset by self-doubt, his leadership was unwaveringly firm; he was *un hombre duro*—a hard man. Political commissar as well as commander, Escalona was the only guerrilla in Pinar del Río capable of making a speech.

After two weeks with Claudio I did not want to switch

to Escalona's group. The Comandante granted my request to remain. The two bands would march together until the night of October 10, when they would split up after an attack on the *cuartel* at Las Pozas.

Since the batistianos claimed that the guerrillas had been annihilated at San Andrés, Escalona felt it necessary to demonstrate his strength. After two days' rest at Claudio's camp, he planned to start back to the west at the head of a combined force of fifty-eight men. The day before we marched we butchered a cow whose meat tasted good after so many days of pork. The beef was fried, and what was not eaten at supper was distributed cold the next day for breakfast. Walking and chewing, it took me all morning to swallow the tough but savory steak.

When Escalona was on the march he was little concerned with eating or sleeping. On the best days we received a cup of hot chocolate in the morning and a plate of rice, sometimes laced with canned beans or tuna, before nightfall. We would walk all day and much of the night. Avoiding roads and decent trails, we plunged through the thickest underbrush—even at night when we must have sounded like a herd of disoriented elephants to anyone within earshot.

As all this went against my military training, I did a lot of grumbling. "One should never march through the forest at night," I remarked pontifically to my companions in the ranks. "It makes too much noise. At night one marches along the roads and across open terrain. And this business of not eating is also very bad. It is necessary to eat regularly in order to keep the soldiers in good spirits. In the Korean War, even during the fiercest fighting, the troops received three good meals a day—one of which was always hot, with meat and vegetables." I was not a veteran of the Korean War, but I spoke so authoritatively about that conflict that everyone believed I was, despite my denials. Cuba, however, was not Korea, and Escalona was right and I was wrong. The Cuban poor, who comprised our army, were not used to eating regularly; missing a few meals had little effect on their morale, which depended not on food but on the prospects for revolutionary success. Food was necessary as fuel for the body but, as I would learn, the human machine will run about as well on weekly stokings as on daily ones. As for tramping through the brush at night, Escalona was insuring against ambush. The enemy might hear us, but he could do little damage to us. He had at his immediate disposal no area weapons—no artillery barrages or air strikes to call down upon us. The batistianos could only hope to learn our direction of march and lay ambushes for us on likely roads or trails. Escalona had been caught in such a trap near San Andrés after a chivato informed the enemy of his location.

Escalona went to great lengths to confuse the batistianos. For hours we waded knee-deep through the swirling waters of a mountain stream. Water filled my Hong Kong walking boots, adding unwelcome weight to my tired legs. I had already lost one heel on the trail; then I lost the other on the rocky creek bottom. When one sole began to flap I realized that I would have to discard my much-admired footware. The next morning I accepted from Claudio a pair of high-topped Cuban work shoes.

We finally halted for an extended rest on the afternoon of October 3. We camped on a wooded slope along one side of a large stream. The next day the Comandante would send foragers out to look for pigs. I fell into my hammock with delightful visions of the coming feast. In the morning, after the usual breakfast of hot chocolate, I cleaned my carbine. Then I turned my attention to a pistol I had acquired the day before we began the march.

The pistol was a .45 caliber Colt's military revolver—exactly like one that as a boy I had bought by mail through an advertisement in the *American Rifleman*. The underground had sent Claudio several pistols of this type, the standard side arm of the Rural Guard regiments of the Cuban Army. Since I displayed such great interest in, and knowledge of, these hand guns, Claudio gave me one. I always made much of my preference for revolvers over automatics; as a teen-ager I had owned a .45 automatic that constantly jammed, and in the army I had never learned to shoot one well. But it was due less to conviction than to natural contrariness that I praised revolvers when I knew Cubans loved automatics.

On the morning of October 4 I removed the cartridges from the revolver and discovered that my trusty six-shooter was on the blink. Something had been jarred loose in the double-action mechanism; the hammer wouldn't go back more than halfway. I stripped off the side plate and gazed at the innards; one part was out of place, but I couldn't put it back where I thought it belonged. I had to check the action of a similar pistol that was in working order. Tite, who was sitting a few yards away with Ramoncito, let me borrow his. With my own pistol in my lap, I removed the side plate from Tite's, pointed it at the boulder in front of me, and slowly pulled the trigger as I studied the movements of the mechanism. There was an almost deafening explosion as the gun went off. The whispered conversations around me stopped as everyone looked in my direction and then quickly turned away.

The silence was broken in less than a minute as Escalona stormed on the scene.

"Who did that?" he demanded of Tite.

"I don't know," he lied.

Before Escalona could look further, I spoke up: "I did it." There was nothing else to say, so I just sat there on my pack, probably looking more defiant than contrite.

Claudio came over and tried to explain for me: "There was this revolver that was broken and the American was trying to fix it. He took this other revolver and . . ."

Escalona turned and walked away and Claudio followed him. Several minutes later Claudio came back and gently informed me that "Escalona says I have to take the revolver." He had not one word of reproach for me.

The next shots we heard that day were fired by Escalona's men down by the creek. An army patrol moving along the stream had walked up on one of our guard posts. The two rebel sentries greeted the enemy with the automatic fire of a Star and a Sten gun. One batistiano fell and the others—perhaps half a dozen in all—beat a hasty retreat. Escalona was of no mind to pursue them. *¡Arriba! ¡Arriba!* he shouted. "Up the hill! Get moving!" We scrambled up the wooded slope to the top of the ridge where we paused only long enough to get into our regular marching order before striking out cross country. There was little underbrush, but the steepness of the terrain made the going difficult. After about an hour we halted for a rest. Up and down the line the men discussed in excited whispers what had happened down at the creek.

During the break Escalona walked up to where I was sitting and asked, "How does it seem to you, americano?"

"To me it seems that we have been beaten by six men."

"You believe that?" He wasn't angry or sarcastic or condescending; he just seemed to regret that I believed it, and that he couldn't set me right at that time.

It was then that someone shouted in his loudest whisper, "¡Avión!" The monotonous drone of a small aircraft could be heard. As it seemed to be growing steadily louder, Escalona sent the order down the line: "Hide yourselves." Through breaks in the forest canopy we could see the plane; it was a Piper Tri-Pacer from the regimental headquarters in Pinar del Río City. The patrol we had fired upon must have contacted it by radio. The plane was methodically searching the valleys and mountainsides, flying only a few feet above the treetops. But we were too well hidden to be seen, even if the plane flew directly above us, which it was going to do.

"Let's knock down the son of a whore," I suggested to Escalona as the Tri-Pacer approached overhead. "He cannot escape if we shoot with all our *ametralladoras* and rifles."

"No, let him go." Escalona, as I was later to learn, was afraid that the plane might survive our fusillade and report our location and firepower to enemy headquarters. If the batistianos found out how much strength he had concentrated in that part of the province, they would take precautions and make it difficult for him to carry out his plans to attack an army barracks on the north coast. But he didn't explain this to me at the time, and my opinion of the Comandante sank to a new low.

We marched through the afternoon and most of the night. The following day we trudged on. We were each given a can of condensed milk for breakfast, and our only other meal of the day consisted of a little brown sugar. That night there were two desertions, and the next morning, October 6, we formed into patrols to hunt down the runaways.

I went with Quintín and Changó. We left our packs where we had slept the night before and climbed to the top of a little knoll. "This looks like a good place to spend the day," Quintín observed. Changó and I agreed, so we stretched out on the ground and lit up cigars. We were seldom without tobacco, although with Escalona we had little time to enjoy it. We spent a pleasant day there on the hilltop—smoking, talking, dozing. We had plenty of water in our canteens and for food we each had a can of condensed milk. This was supplemented by some *mamoncillos*—wild berries—that Changó found growing nearby. Late that afternoon we returned to camp with our story of no success in the search. A more conscientious patrol from Escalona's band had caught the deserters, two high-school boys from Pinar del Río City. They had been hanged and were already in their graves when we reported in.

After that Escalona eased up. For supper we cooked all the rice we had and everyone got a fairly decent serving, which was garnished with a little *tasajo*, or canned jerked beef. We were on the march again the following morning, but the pace was slower than before. There was little to eat during the day, but word came down from the Comandante that we would sup well that night. When the sun set we were still on the trail.

At about eight o'clock we descended into a beautiful little valley. Much of the land was cultivated. To one side of the hollow, where a small brook splashed down from the mountain, was a clump of coconut palms and fruit trees. Among the trees, illuminated by a kerosene lantern, was a neat and well-built farm house. It was the home of *buena gente,* good people: an industrious mulatto and his son who welcomed Escalona with a joyous effusion worthy of a resurrected messiah. Aided by Escalona's expert cooks and butchers, the man and his son immediately went to work preparing a feast.

In the meantime Claudio encamped his men on the mountainside above the house. I hung my hammock near a miniature dam which formed a reservoir that supplied water through a bamboo aqueduct to the dwelling below. In the valley they were slitting the throats of pigs whose dying squeals, I must say, were delightful to hear. Soon the delicious smell of boiling lard rose to our nostrils. Every pot and cauldon in the house, along with all those carried by the guerrillas, were used to fry the food: pork, plantains, and breadfruit. Our host apologized for being unable to offer us rice but said that he would roast some *yuca*— a starchy root—in the embers after the frying was done.

It was nearly midnight before we could file past the cookfires and fill our tin plates. A waning half-moon rose over the valley and cast down a glorious light for dining. We ate for hours, every man refilling his plate several times. More pigs were slaughtered, more plantains thrown into the bubbling cauldrons. The water of the brook, naturally chilled to the perfect temperature, enhanced the joy of an incomparable meal. After about three hours of continuous eating, I could hold no more. I tumbled into my hammock and fell right off to sleep. In less than two hours I awoke and, to my surprise, discovered that I was hungry again. I rejoined my comrades and resumed the meal which lasted past sunrise and, in fact, continued intermittently throughout the next morning.

We left our hammocks hanging all that day and by afternoon most of us were snoozing like sated lions. This luxury, however, was denied our Comandante and his staff, who spent the afternoon fetching and inventorying supplies. With our host's horses, they brought from somewhere nearby cases of La Lechera condensed milk; cases of canned fruit, meat, and black beans; huge sacks of rice marked "Produce of Arkansas"; and five-gallon containers of kerosene for our cookstoves. There were even a few bottles of Bacardi rum. That night these goods were distributed to the men for carrying.

When we marched the next day our packs were heavy, but our strength had been restored and we hardly noticed the added burdens. We stopped at noon to cook and eat rice; in mid-afternoon we paused again. As we sat along a shaded path, two bottles of rum were passed from each end of our line to the middle. There was a good slug for everyone who wanted it; only a few devout evangelical Protestants in Escalona's group abstained. Later in the afternoon we camped on a high mountain from which we could see the Gulf of Mexico.

At breakfast on the morning of October 10, Claudio told

us that we would attack that night. Escalona soon appeared before us to confirm the news. Claudio's group would assault a *cuartel* while Escalona's men would wait in ambush for possible enemy reinforcements. The Comandante was accompanied by Cienfueguero, his tommy-gun-toting aide, and a skinny old man whom I had seen before with Escalona's group. The old man marched with a full pack, but he didn't wear a uniform and never carried a weapon. He was a *chivato*, an informer, whom Escalona's guerrillas had captured near San Andrés.

"It is because your people have shown such high spirits," the Comandante told Claudio, "that I decided that you should initiate the action. And I have another job for you: to do away with this *cabrón*."

"No," the old man pleaded. *Yo no hablo*—"I do not talk." He wore a tattered sleeveless undershirt and a pair of grey cotton pants; the seam of one trouser leg was split from the knee to the crotch, and I noticed that he was wearing a truss. In a moment Pipilo and Pancho appeared with a rope and pushed the chivato before them toward a low-hanging limb. He continued to mutter *Yo no hablo* as Pipilo fixed the noose around his neck and Pancho tossed the rest of the rope over the limb. Without a second of delay and without a word, the two executioners grabbed the free end of the rope and suddenly pulled the chivato three feet off the ground. It was a quick, graceful movement. The man did not kick or thrash about. One moment he was alive and talking, the next he was dead, his eyes closed and his head tilted to one side. Pancho and Pipilo tied the free end of the rope to the trunk of a nearby tree to keep his body suspended while Quintín and El Indio dug his grave.

Pipilo began teasing Changó, trying to get him to touch the dead man. But Changó refused to go near the hanging corpse. "Changó has fear of the dead," Pipilo said with a grin. Then he looked at me.

"Hey, americano, do you have fear of the dead?"

"Of the dead I have no fear," I answered. "The only people whom I fear are alive."

3 ESCALONA TOOK ORDERS ONLY FROM
Fidel's headquarters in the Sierra Maestra. These orders
had to be delivered and acknowledged by messenger, for
there was no two-way radio contact between the rebels in
Oriente and Pinar del Río provinces. Escalona, however,
did have a short-wave receiver—a magnificent Zenith
Transoceanic that he had appropriated from the home of
some informer—and he could keep abreast of the situation
elsewhere on the island by tuning in the nightly broadcasts
of *Radio Rebelde* from the Sierra Maestra. Whenever possible I joined those who gathered around the Comandante's
radio to hear the transmissions from Oriente.

In early October, Radio Rebelde reported on the progress of two fidelista columns that had been marching west-
ward from the Sierra Maestra. They had crossed Camagüey
and were now in Las Villas province. One column, commanded by Comandante Ernesto "Che" Guevara, had
linked up with the guerrillas who had long been operating
in the Sierra del Escambray. When Escalona sent us to
attack Las Pozas on October 10, I surmised that he was
under orders to demonstrate sufficient strength in Pinar
del Río to make Batista reluctant to commit his reserves in
Havana to the front in Las Villas.

We were encamped near the summit of Pan de Guajaibón, the highest mountain in western Cuba with an elevation of 2,388 feet. Before noon we began to move down and eastward along the mountain's northern face toward Las Pozas. In mid-afternoon we crossed a spur and entered a clearing. From there we could see the little town of Las Pozas; it was on the black-topped highway that ran along the plain between the sierra and the Gulf of Mexico, whose waters sparkled on the horizon. At that vantage point, about two miles from our objective, we halted.

I climbed on a big rock in the clearing for a better view of the town we were going to invade. Then Escalona appeared and joined me on the rock; it was the platform from which he intended to make a speech to Claudio's band. It didn't occur to me that I should step down, so I remained there at the chief's side while he harangued Claudio and the men assembled below. After reminding us of our duty to the Revolution, Escalona pointed out that the Movement had furnished us the tools to accomplish our mission; besides good rifles, we had five hand grenades, four tommy guns, one fully automatic carbine, two semi-automatic carbines, and, the Comandante said as he made a flourish in the direction of the character standing next to him, *un americano con cojones*—"an American with balls."

The *cuartel*, which housed a Rural Guard platoon, was on the highway at the eastern outskirts of Las Pozas. October 10 was a holiday, the anniversary of the *Grito de Yara*, Cuba's cry for independence from Spain in 1868. We expected most of the enemy soldiers to be away celebrating when we attacked their barracks that night.

After an early supper in the clearing on the lower slope of the mountain, we resumed our march to the east. It was not long before we came to a dirt road; there we took up ambush positions and waited for night to fall. During the wait some civilian vehicles came by which we stopped and appropriated. Shortly after 7:30 we left our packs and the occupants of the commandeered vehicles under the guard of Cucalambé and Sosa, the medic, and moved north along the dirt road toward the central highway. The Comandante and about half his men led the way in a Chevrolet sedan and two jeeps; the rest of his band, led by Captain Pepito, followed on foot. Claudio's group, also on foot, brought up the rear. It was barely a mile to the junction of the dirt road and the highway, and only about a hundred yards east of there to the cuartel.

At the junction Escalona turned right to lay an ambush on the highway. Pepito's and Claudio's men went off to the left and began to crawl toward the cuartel, which stood on the north side of the highway. There was no moon and it was almost pitch black. Claudio's seventeen guerrillas, who included one tommy-gunner detached from Escalona's group, formed a semi-circle around the front and the near side of the squat, concrete structure; Pepito meanwhile led his men past it, to guard the approach from town. The attack commenced promptly at eight o'clock.

Lying in a shallow ditch directly in front of the cuartel's main door, Claudio opened fire with a burst from his San Cristóbal automatic carbine. The rest of the band immediately joined in. The guerrillas at the side of the building poked their rifle muzzles through the windows and fired into the living quarters. Three grenades were tossed into the dormitory but none went off. From in front of the building I rolled a grenade up against the main door; then I tried to throw another through the window of the adjacent guard room. Neither exploded. Lying prone on an asphalt driveway about twenty feet in front of the guard room, I could hear someone inside frantically cranking a telephone. I put a few shots through the window and was answered by a burst of automatic fire that produced dancing sparks on the pavement a few inches from my face. It persuaded me to retreat behind a concrete post several feet away.

We had intended to storm the building when the grenades went off. But the failure of this underground-loaded ordnance converted the attack into a siege. For twenty minutes we splattered the concrete walls of the cuartel with small-arms fire while verbally assaulting the defenders with obscenities and revolutionary slogans. After nearly four weeks of whispering, it felt good to use my lungs again and yell *¡Viva la Revolución!* It seemed appropriate to let the enemy hear a little English, too, like "Batista eats shit!"

One of us would shout *¡Ríndanse, maricones!*—"Surrender, queers!"—and there would be a pause in our firing. But the enemy would not respond, so soon someone would cry *¡Viva Fidel Castro!*, and the cheer would be punctuated with a tremendous rebel fusillade. Two or three times Claudio called to the batistianos to surrender, omitting the insults and assuring them of good treatment. The enemy replied with gunfire.

I noticed that our captain was shooting with his automatic pistol. His San Cristóbal carbine had jammed, which, I thought, was to be expected of something produced by Trujillo's Dominican Republic. But one of our Thompson submachine guns, made in the U.S.A., was also out of action, its barrel split like the peel of a banana.

Claudio called me over to tell me that Escalona had instructed him to withdraw after twenty minutes, when Pepito's men were due to pass the cuartel. He asked my advice on how best to break off the engagement. I suggested that he let me cover the withdrawal. With a thirty-round magazine in my carbine, I could maintain a steady fire and keep batistiano heads down for a minute or two, allowing our people to slip away and fall in behind Pepito's troops on the highway. When this was accomplished, I would make a dash to join Claudio's rear guard. The captain agreed, urging me not to remain in my position a second too long.

From behind the concrete post I fired at the windows on the front and on the side of the cuartel. As my comrades moved away, I noticed that one man was being carried. There were still five cartridges in my magazine when I decided that the time had come for me to break contact. I squeezed the trigger for a parting shot and—nothing happened; I pulled on the operating handle, but it wouldn't budge. After firing nearly two hundred times, the carbine was sizzling hot and jammed tight.

Clutching the useless weapon I ran to the highway, slowing down to a fast walk as I fell in with Pancho and El Habanero. "This piece of shit is not functioning," I muttered, jerking on the operating handle as I walked along. My rear-guard companions paid me little attention as they moved briskly down the side of the highway, constantly looking back over their shoulders at the cuartel.

¡Ay—mi mamá! El Habanero shouted as he bolted and began to scramble up the vine-covered bank on the side of the road.

"A truck full of *guardias!*" Pancho yelled ahead as he followed El Habanero up the bank.

There was indeed an army truck bearing down on us with someone firing from the right window of the cab. I cursed my useless carbine and dove to the ground just before the vehicle roared past. Up the line only two or three shots were fired at it. I could hear Claudio yelling, *¡Coño!* "Fire! Fire!" *¡Coño!* The truck successfully ran the gantlet past the troops of Claudio, Pepito, and Escalona. I later learned that it was driven by a sergeant determined to carry a wounded comrade to a doctor in Bahía Honda. When the firing at the cuartel had stopped the sergeant lost no time in loading his buddy on a truck in the adjoining garage and, with one man riding shotgun, made his dash through the rebel lines. Claudio's band inflicted only this single casualty on the batistianos, while one of our men, Tite, was seriously wounded in the chest. But the overall score for that night favored the fidelistas: Just after the shooting started at the cuartel, one enemy soldier was killed driving his jeep into Escalona's ambush.

At the junction of the highway and the dirt road, Tite was lifted onto the back seat of a jeep and driven where we had left our packs. There Sosa gave the wounded man an injection of morphine. A small tree was chopped down and a pole about ten feet long was fashioned from its trunk. It was in a hammock slung under the pole that we carried Tite halfway up Pan de Guajaibón. The burden was shouldered by four men at a time, with Escalona's troops and Claudio's both taking their turns. Although each bearer supported little more than forty pounds, the load seemed heavier because it was concentrated on one shoulder. The wounded man appeared unconscious but occasionally, when a bearer stumbled and jostled him, he would emit a low moan. To prevent further injury to our comrade, we used flashlights to illuminate the trail.

About midnight we arrived at a cave, where we left Tite in the care of Sosa. Escalona dispatched one of his men to the lowland to fetch a doctor, then set out with the remainder of his band for the mountains to the south-west. Our group turned toward the southeast. There was some rain before dawn. About six o'clock we hung our hammocks on a wooded peak. I lost no sleep on account of my carbine. While walking I had field-stripped the weapon, returning the slide to the track it had jumped; it now seemed to be working perfectly.

About noon the next day a pair of B-25's from Havana flew over and made several bombing runs on a mountain some two miles west of us. We knew no one was there. If by chance they had chosen to bomb where we were they wouldn't have hurt us much. Our campsite was strewn with huge basalt boulders which could protect us pretty well from blasts and shrapnel. When the planes first appeared we selected and settled in these individual bomb shelters. After the aircraft flew away, we returned to the business of drying the clothes and equipment that had been soaked by the rain the night before.

We had little protection against the rain when we marched. Each man had a sheet of waterproof plastic or oilcloth in which he could wrap his hammock and some clothes before putting them into his pack. But anything worn or carried on the person was bound to get drenched. Before we attacked the cuartel I removed my passport from my pack and put it in a pocket; on the morning after, it was soaked. The same was true of $5,000 in Cuban currency that Claudio had stuffed into his pockets before the attack. On one big sunny rock, hundred-peso bills and a United States passport lay drying next to socks and underwear.

My comrades were intrigued by the passport. "Is this uniform you are wearing in the photograph that of the Army of the United States?" Ramoncito asked.

"No, it is the uniform of a military academy called The Citadel, which I attended before entering the army."

¡Coño! Ramoncito exclaimed as he flipped past visas for Cambodia and Taiwan. "Look at this writing."

"There is also a visa that was written personally by the dictator of Nicaragua," I pointed out, and quickly added, "although the truth is that I am not a friend of his."

"Americano," Pipilo said with a wink and a grin, *tú eres un bicho.*

"You have walked over the world," Claudio said. I admitted that I was an inveterate tourist. Neither the captain nor any of his Cuban subordinates had ever left their native country. I realized then that they formed a class quite distinct from the urbane exiles in New York and the English-speaking revolutionaries in Havana.

The Cuban guerrilla movement, which had been gaining momentum since Fidel repulsed Batista's Sierra Maestra offensive in July, became irresistible in the fall. The independent underground organizations, which had recognized the 26 of July guerrillas as the vanguard of the Revolution by accepting Fidel's terms for collaboration during the summer, were now providing financial assistance to the fidelistas in the sierras. Funds were also raised by the guerrillas themselves, who levied a tax of fifteen cents on every bag of sugar produced during 1958 in Oriente, Cuba's richest agricultural province, most of which was under rebel control. Money from Oriente was sent to Las Villas and Pinar del Río to support guerrilla activity in those provinces.

Nearly two years of fruitless operations against the guerrillas had infected Batista's soldiers in Oriente with a defensive malaise. They retired from the countryside to the cities and larger towns, fighting only when attacked. In the fall of 1958 the disease spread to government troops in Las Villas and, finally, to those in Pinar del Río. Nevertheless, the enemy in our province was by no means disabled; certainly, every member of Claudio's band retained a healthy respect for him. Those from Havana had witnessed the crushing efficiency with which the dictator's forces broke the general strike of April 9. We all knew that Escalona's group had been aggressively pursued at San Andrés. The six-man patrol that invaded the mountains on October 4, the crew of the Tri-Pacer that flew over our heads, and the batistianos in the truck who charged through our lines at Las Pozas were not without cojones. We had little reason to believe that the enemy would not pursue us after Las Pozas.

Claudio's mission was, first, to survive, which meant eluding and if possible destroying any pursuing soldiers; and, second, to bring the entire population of the highlands east of Pan de Guajaibón under rebel control. Once all the batistianos and chivatos were cleared out of the mountains, he could begin striking into the lowlands. Claudio was given a zone of responsibility stretching from

Bahía Honda and San Cristóbal on the west to the border of Havana province on the east. Our outfit operated closer to the Cuban capital than any other guerrilla band. To the west of us, Escalona assigned territory to Pepito on the north and Captain Antonio on the south. The Comandante set up his general headquarters in a cave in the Sierra de los Órganos south of La Palma.

The limestone cordillera of Pinar del Río is separated into two ranges by the Valley of San Diego de los Baños. The more spectacular is the one on the west, the Sierra de los Órganos, which has masses of blue-black limestone that rise vertically from flat-floored valleys like giant haystacks. These are the *mogotes*, the oldest geological formations in Cuba. Millions of years of rain and wind have rounded their peaks, carrying away the softer limestone at their bases; their surfaces are riddled with caves and sinks and crisscrossed with crevices. These grooves collect soil and from them sprouts a unique vegetation—dragon trees, sierra palms, cayman oaks—that gives the mogotes the appearance of enormous sponges. After the skirmish at San Andrés, Pepito led the remnants of Escalona's band to the top of Elephant mogote. The pursuing batistianos blocked off the Elephant's trunk and tail, but the rebels eluded the enemy by tying their hammocks together and lowering themselves down the mogote's most precipitous side.

In elevation the highlands of Pinar del Río barely qualify as mountains. Although the mogotes are impressive and in other parts of the cordillera there are peaks that rise more than two thousand feet above the nearby sea, the most striking feature of the whole upland region is its forest cover. The peasants who live there call it *el monte*—which means woods, not mountain. On the northern flank of the Órganos range are the shale hills that once supported the extensive stands of pine for which the province was named. Greedy lumbermen ravaged the pine lands but left largely untouched the forests of the Sierra de los Órganos and its continuation to the east, the Sierra del Rosario. The coveted pine did not grow in the calcareous soil of the sierras, while the trees that did were generally of less commercial value. The steepness of the terrain made lumbering operations difficult along with precluding large-scale farming; so the natural vegetation of the sierras of Pinar del Río survived and, in the 1950's, constituted Cuba's largest forest west of Las Villas.

Although the highlands of Pinar del Río receive more rain than any other region of Cuba—from sixty-five to ninety inches annually—the precipitation is seasonal, which prevents the development of a true tropical rainforest. Many trees in the province shed leaves during the dry season, which runs from December through April. A period of regular rains begins in May and lasts through the summer; hurricane activity prolongs the wet season into the autumn. About 75 per cent of the annual rainfall in Pinar del Río occurs between May and November.

Except for the mogotes, with their unique vegetation, the Órganos range has a forest cover identical to that of the adjacent Sierra del Rosario. The trees grow close together, generally tall and straight—some reach one hundred feet—with small leaves and relatively limited spreads of foliage. Many are hardwoods, like the *yaba*, the *sabicú*, and the *dagame*, which the Indians preferred for making their bows. But the forest also has its leafy, low-slung *algarrobos* and malevolent strangler figs, with roots descending from their trunks like the tentacles of an octopus.

Occasionally, a giant *ceiba* stands alone, with its elephantine trunk and spreading branches—a sacred tree to the extinct aborigines who spun cloth with silk cotton extracted from its seedpods. Vines hang from above and saplings rise up between the larger trunks, but neither obstructs passage through the forest. In fact, small trees facilitated our descent of many a steep slope: with rifle in one hand, a guerrilla could use the other to swing from sapling to sapling, and thus regulate his downhill speed.

Wild fruit, especially guavas and *mamoncillos*, were found in the woods, and there was also some game. Deer were occasionally seen, but the *jutía*, a tree rodent, was much more common. This animal could be captured alive by anyone skilled in tree climbing; its flesh tasted more like rabbit than squirrel. The meat most consumed by the guerrillas, however, was pork. Some of the pigs we slaughtered were wild, but most belonged to the peasants who lived in clearings where they cultivated patches of *malanga* and *yuca* and left their swine free to root in the forest around them. Whenever we killed a pig we made every effort to find its owner and compensate him. For an average-sized animal we gave twenty dollars, which was far above the market price. Our generosity won us many friends.

During the summer Claudio had built a strong base of support among the peasants of the northern slopes of the Sierra del Rosario, from Bahía Honda to Cabañas. In October, after the skirmish at Las Pozas, we crossed to the southern slopes to extend our control over the area above San Cristóbal and Candelaria. For me the march across the sierra was especially difficult. A thorn had punctured my knee when I crawled into position before the attack on the cuartel; for thirty-six hours I experienced only minor discomfort, but by the third day my knee had swollen to twice its normal size and was throbbing painfully. That afternoon my comrades relieved me of my pack; and when we stopped for the night I began to experience chills and fever. Since our antibiotics were in the cave with Sosa and Tite, the only medicine available was aspirin. This, though, relieved the fever and much of the pain, and on the fourth day the swelling began to subside to the point where I was able to continue the march. I knew the outfit couldn't halt on account of me. We didn't even stop to celebrate the "Day of the Race," as Columbus Day is called in Cuba. Claudio postponed observance of this important Hispanic holiday until we reached our destination across the sierra.

We made contact with friendly peasants north of San Cristóbal, where we belatedly celebrated *el Día de la Raza* with roast pork, yuca, beer, and rum. The roast pork—*lechón asado*—was traditional for festive occasions. It tasted better than our usual fried pork and we consumed enormous quantities of it, along with more than a gallon of rum and countless bottles of cool beer. The fiesta began in late afternoon, continuing past midnight. We were in a secure location, surrounded by friends, and Claudio could let us lie in our hammocks the next day to sleep off the effects of the celebration.

My admiration for our captain continued to grow. Escalona, I felt, would never have permitted us to consume so much alcohol; some tipsy guerrilla might have found the courage to tell him to go to hell—or even to take a shot at him. But Claudio had instilled in the band a spirit of voluntary discipline that made such behavior inconceivable, even when the men were completely drunk. We all liked Claudio and, more important, respected him. There was never any doubt that the captain was the best man among us; no resentment agitated the minds of the peasants and workers who followed him. We accepted his decisions automatically, usually without comment. The only grumbling I remember was done by El Habanero, the bus driver, who once mumbled some protests as we began moving through a stretch of open country during daylight. When Claudio at the head of the column heard of the dissent in the ranks, he stopped, turned around, and called out: "Habanero, I am going to shit on your mother!" That was the only time I heard him use insulting language toward one of the men. In this case it was justified and effective; the griping stopped and we crossed the dangerous ground quickly and without further incident.

Claudio had the good sense not to carry out all orders to the letter. There was no question of his complete subordination to Escalona; the captain merely realized that the Comandante's objectives could be more easily attained if some of his instructions were disregarded. Claudio's attitude was the traditional Spanish *obedezco pero no cumplo* —"I obey but I do not comply." Escalona had declared that every able-bodied member of the Rebel Army was bound to service for the duration of the conflict. Claudio nevertheless decided to release Cucalambé after we marched over the mountains from Las Pozas. Cucalambé wasn't cut out to be a guerrilla. He was no goldbrick—he conscientiously tried to do all that we required of him and rarely complained—but the hardships of the last three weeks had transformed his early euphoria into a deepening melancholia. It was best for him and for the outfit that he be sent home. We were all touched with sadness as we said goodbye to our comrade.

We spent two weeks getting to know the people and the terrain of the sierra above San Cristóbal and Candelaria, and we accepted some recruits from the area. The loss of Cucalambé had reduced our number to fifteen; from this low number it would rise to forty-six before the end of the year. The numerical increase was not necessarily desirable. Few of the newcomers brought usable weapons; moreover, they made movement more difficult and added greatly to our logistical problems. But most were wanted by the police for revolutionary activity in the lowland, and, since we couldn't deny them refuge, we welcomed them as comrades. Occasionally a mountain peasant would join our ranks, but we still preferred that the peasants of the sierra remain at home where they could perform support functions. The peasants were enrolled in the Rebel Army militia and told that they would be called to active service at the right moment. In the meantime they purchased and stored supplies for us and served as guides when needed.

The *guajiros* were almost unanimously ardent fidelistas. Successive Cuban governments had done little for them; they had been left to raise their families in ignorance and misery. They knew there was a better way of life and now at last it was being promised to them—not by obese politicians on a swing through the hinterland, but by young men who demonstrated their sincerity by living among them and enduring hardships as great as their own. The peasants trusted the guerrillas and joined them in the struggle for liberation; virtually the only exceptions were the chivatos—those who were paid by the government to inform on their neighbors.

The most notorious of these informers in our part of the sierra lived beside a paved road that knifed into the mountains from the central highway between San Cristóbal and Candelaria. His house was about a mile below Soroa, a scenic spot that was the terminus of the road. A billboard announced that the Jack Tar chain of the United States was going to build a hotel in Soroa, but in 1958 the place had only a park with a waterfall, two or three houses, and a bar and restaurant. The peasants of the area feared the informer, and they became quite uneasy when they spotted police or army cars traveling along the paved road. The batistianos usually were only on their way to the restaurant in Soroa. Nevertheless, even these innocent visits to the sierra by the police and military could no longer be tolerated. And, of course, the informer had to be eliminated. On Halloween night we would drive the enemy out of Soroa.

We had acquired no ammunition to replace what we had shot up at the cuartel. Those of us with .30 caliber carbines—Claudio, Alberto, and I—pooled our cartridges and then divided them equally: eighty for each of us. Several rifles of odd calibers had to be abandoned because there was no ammunition for them. The heaviest weapons brought by the newcomers were a few shotguns with about a dozen shells apiece. We had fewer than two hundred rounds apiece for our three Thompson submachine guns. The barrel of Mateo's tommy gun had split about six inches from the muzzle, but with a hacksaw we sawed off the ruptured portion and pronounced the abbreviated weapon serviceable. Claudio decided to send tommy-gunners Pipilo and Mateo with Serafín, our peasant guide, to the informer's house while the rest of us occupied Soroa and its bar-restaurant.

Late in the afternoon of October 31 we moved to a peak overlooking Soroa, from where we could see the restaurant. It was built on a curve and was open on the two sides facing the road. There wasn't much activity down there in the afternoon, but as it began to get dark business picked up. Several cars pulled into the parking area, and by eight o'clock there were at least a dozen customers seated at the tables or standing at the bar. The place was brightly illuminated with the first electric lights we had seen in three weeks. The jukebox alternated in playing cha-cha-chas and Mexican mariachi music. We converged on the place at 8:30.

We emerged from the darkness, charging across the road in a skirmish line. Some of us raced up the steps to the dining area, others vaulted over the rails on the two open sides. The people in the restaurant received us bearded intruders in stunned silence. A guerrilla had yanked out the jukebox plug and the only sounds were fidelista commands: *¡Arriba! ¡Manos arriba!* Slowly the customers began to rise from their chairs with their hands above their heads. The men were lined up against the wall and searched, the women put under guard at one table. On Claudio's order, I took three men and set up an outpost a hundred yards down the road.

As I walked down the steps followed by Quintín, Changó, and Pancho, I saw a man coming out of the restroom.

"Halt! Hands up!" I ordered, aiming my carbine from the hip.

"Ah, you are fidelistas," the man said, as he continued to stroll toward us.

"Hold it! Raise those hands or I am going to shoot!"

"*Ol rait, ol rait.*" He calmly pronounced the Cuban adaptation of "all right" as he raised his hands to chest level, but he didn't stop walking. With his thumbs and index fingers he pinched his sport shirt and raised it above his waist. "See, I do not have a weapon." He finally stopped about three feet from me.

"You are an americano. What a good rifle you have. Let me see it, *chico.*"

The son of a bitch was trying to disarm me, I thought. Either that or he was the world's prize idiot. There I was with a fully loaded carbine pointed at his gut, a six-week growth of beard, a filthy green uniform, a black beret cocked at a jaunty angle, and two Negro killers standing at my side—and this clown was asking for a closer look at my gun. I flipped off the safety and it made an audible click.

"Señor, if you do not raise your hands above your head, I am going to kill you." My voice quavered because I didn't want to do it.

"*O qué, ol rait,*" he muttered as he put up his hands.

"Very well," I said with a great relief. "Now you have to go over there where the others are."

As I watched him join the prisoners who were being searched by Alberto and Mesa, I resolved never to let anyone do that to me again. It was stupid and undignified for me to stand there threatening to shoot him. I should have swung my carbine around and given him a vertical butt stroke and smash, as I had learned to do in bayonet practice at Fort Benning, Georgia.

It wasn't long after I positioned my three men along the road that we heard firing in the distance. There were some single shots and then a burst of submachine gun fire.

"They are having problems with the informer," Pancho surmised. The firing did not last long. Twenty minutes after it stopped we made out three forms, very close together, slowly moving up the center of the road. Pipilo gave the bird call that was the fidelista password.

Pipilo and Mateo were supporting Serafín, the guide, who was hopping on one foot. Mateo's sawed-off tommy gun was slung across his back, his left arm was hanging limp at his side. They told us what had happened: as Serafín walked up to the house to lure the informer out, somebody inside began shooting and hit the guide in the leg. Pipilo and Mateo then opened up on the house with their tommy guns. The chivato escaped through a window, but his wife was killed. Mateo's hands—especially his left hand, which he used to steady his weapon by grasping the magazine—were badly burned by the gas blow-back of the altered submachine gun.

Because Serafín's wound was serious, Claudio decided not to move him any further. If we carried him with us into the forest, he would lose more blood and probably end up with gangrene. Better to hide him near the road and send word of his whereabouts to Dr. Triana, a member of the Movement in San Cristóbal, who should be able to reach him the next morning. Of course, there was also a chance that the batistianos would find him. But Claudio was confident that the enemy wouldn't mistreat Serafín.

Three of the men we captured in the restaurant turned out to be members of the Cuban National Police, and one of the three was the son of the batistiano mayor of Candelaria. To insure decent treatment for Serafín we would take them with us as hostages.

The man who had asked to see my carbine wasn't among the hostages. I was glad because I didn't want to see him again.

4   THE BATISTIANOS FOUND SERAFÍN. A peasant brought the news to our camp on the afternoon after the Soroa raid. We had not moved far the preceding night, since we intended to stay in the area until the enemy had conceded that part of the sierra to us; with our three hostages we were sure that the Rural Guard wouldn't pursue us. When Claudio learned of Serafín's capture, he sent a peasant to Candelaria with a note for the mayor. If the mayor wanted to see his son alive again, the message said, he had to guarantee good treatment for Serafín; and that meant that the wounded fidelista couldn't be moved from Candelaria, where the mayor—and our agents—could keep an eye on him. The mayor agreed and he fulfilled his promise. When Serafín was liberated from the Candelaria jail on January 1, he was reasonably healthy and could walk, although with a limp.

Padrón, the mayor's son, was a short thin man of about thirty. On the night of his capture he and the other two policemen were told that they would have to answer for their crimes. Padrón with considerable dignity denied committing any crimes, declaring his conscience clear. His eyes were those of a man who had a conscience. Padrón's fellow prisoners were a chubby white man in his twenties

and Aniseto, a wiry Negro in his mid-forties. All three
had been armed. From Aniseto we got only a decrepit .38
revolver, but Padrón gave up a magnificent long-barrel
Luger and the other policeman yielded a new .38 automatic.
Another .38 automatic was taken from the body of the
informer's wife. Neither Pipilo nor Mateo regretted her
death, and Alberto, who sometimes billed himself as *el hijo
de Nena,* agreed with them. "The little children I respect
and will not harm," declared Nena's son. "The children
are not responsible. But why should we respect the women
of these informers? They are worse than the men."

Halloween night convinced most of the informers that
it was time for them to move out of the sierra. But there
were a few who remained, and one of these was a little man
named Benito who lived alone in a *bohío.* One night early
in November Benito was ordered outside his hut by Alberto and three other guerrillas who posed as government
soldiers. When the phony batistianos accused him of being a revolutionary, Benito tried to defend himself by
listing the many things he had done for the dictatorship.
He even claimed that his brother had gone to the Sierra
Maestra to earn the $100,000 reward the government was
offering for the head of Fidel Castro. When Alberto re-
vealed his and his comrades' true identity, Benito didn't
retract anything he had said. He was slow-witted, perhaps
even mentally retarded.

Our prisoners, including Benito, were under guard at all
times. At night their hands and feet were tied. Otherwise
their physical discomfort was not greater than that of
their captors. They received the same food, in the same
portions, as the guerrillas. The three policemen had not

expected to live many hours after their capture, and were greatly cheered upon surviving a full day in captivity. They soon began making friends among the fidelistas. Benito, however, remained sullen and alone.

But he was not with us long, for he was hanged after two days. It was a bungled job, and those present cried out in horror as the hapless little man danced on toes that barely touched the ground and tugged at the noose that was choking him to death. Three guerrillas jerked him a foot higher and there he died, his face frozen in a grotesque popeyed stare. Aniseto, who was eager to help, cut the rope, and he and El Indio carried the body to a nearby sinkhole and heaved it in. The black policeman displayed great energy in rolling big rocks in on top of the corpse to seal the tomb. I wondered how many times he had performed such services for Batista.

Claudio learned that one Captain Iturriaga, who commanded a company of Rural Guards at Bahía Honda, was boasting that he was going to cross the sierra and wipe out the bandits who were terrorizing Soroa. Claudio decided to march north and meet Iturriaga halfway. We crossed the watershed and, early one morning, set up an ambush on a dirt road that entered the mountains from near Bahía Honda. Trucks from Iturriaga's garrison had been seen turning off the northern highway onto the road several days before. We assumed that this was the route he planned to take into the sierra. We mined the road with dynamite, but nobody knew much about explosives, and

I doubted that our corroded electrical equipment would set off the charge. In any case, it was not needed: the soldiers did not appear. Late in the afternoon, however, a lone horseman approached our ambush position. The rider, a tall, skinny mulatto, was immediately recognized as an informer. He was captured and hung on the spot, and his riderless horse was chased down the road toward Bahía Honda. A pair of beautiful *mameyes* that had been found in his saddlebags provided that night's dessert.

If Captain Iturriaga had any serious intentions of invading the sierra, he lost them when he lost this informer. By the second week in November we knew that our control over the monte was complete and incontestable. Our prisoners also noticed the impotence of the government forces, and were impressed by the support we received from the peasants. Before long they realized that the rebels had a good chance of overthrowing the dictatorship. Within a week they had given their word not to try to escape, and we stopped binding their hands and feet at night. All three knew that they were safer with us than they would be anywhere else in Cuba; if they escaped from the sierra, they would be marked for assassination by the revolutionaries in the lowland. Padrón was aware that if he ran away he would be signing his father's death warrant as well as his own. The prisoners remained in camp with the recruits while Claudio led his seasoned and better-armed guerrillas on forays into the sugar cane land at the edge of the forest.

The sugar country between the sierra and the northeastern coast of Pinar del Río was divided into two fiefdoms: that of the Cuban-American Sugar Refining

Company, which operated the Mercedita mill near Cabañas; and that of the Cuban Casanova family, which owned the Orozco mill near Bahía Honda. Each mill—or *central*, as it was called locally—was the hub of a network of roads, lanes, oxcart trails, and narrow-gauge railways which link the fields to the factory. Caught in this web were the *colonos*, the sugar cane farmers, and a rural proletariat of landless peasants. Some of the colonos owned the land they worked, others held leases from the *central* which were non-cancellable as long as the farmers supplied sugar cane to the mill. In a good year, when the prices offered by the mill were high, a colono could pay off some of his debts and perhaps even buy some luxuries —a radio, say, or a kerosene refrigerator, or a stove. The peasants without land could look forward to only three or four months of continuous employment during the harvest season, and hope that they would be able to make enough money then to keep their families alive for the rest of the year.

The peasants of the sugar lands lived in misery more appalling than that of their brethren in the sierra. Their bohíos were usually clustered together in wretched hamlets at the edge of the cane fields, where the water was contaminated and even the most rudimentary sanitary facilities were absent. They were plagued by malaria and intestinal diseases, their children were consumed by parasites. Few attended school, and nobody bothered to teach them the elementary rules of health. All suffered from malnutrition, subsisting most of the year on yuca. Only during the harvest season could they afford foods with protein— rice, beans, perhaps a little meat—and this enabled them to work long hours under the tropical sun. During the rest of the year, *el tiempo muerto,* or the dead time, they led a lethargic existence which was hardly better than death. After the fall of Batista a middle-class Cuban lady would tell me that Fidel was *loco* to try to help the peasants, because they were very lazy.

The squalor of the sugar country was not apparent as we surveyed the land from a peak above Bahía Honda. "Have you ever seen a *pasaje* more beautiful?" El Gallego asked. No, I had not. Softly undulating waves of green cane rolled from the foot of our mountain to the edge of the Deep Bay. Darker vegetation trimmed the shoreline. The horizon divided the blue of the sky from the deeper blue of the Gulf of Mexico. Wavy lines of royal palms traced the courses of streams that meandered through the sugar cane toward the *bahía.* Out near the bay, beyond the last cane field, was the country home that ex-President Prío built with money stolen from the government. We couldn't see Prío's *finca,* but to the east the tall, white smoke stack of the Orozco mill was clearly visible, and farther away we saw another bahía, the Bay of Cabañas. The fields in that area belonged to the Mercedita mill, which lay hidden from our sight in some fold in the distant cane-covered terrain.

During the next two weeks, mostly at night, we walked the lands of the Casanovas and the Cuban-American Sugar Refining Company. From bases in the sierra we could reach any point in the cane country in one night and return to camp before dawn. Without our packs we could easily cover twenty-five miles between dawn and sunrise, marching down fire lanes, along roads and railroad tracks.

The peasants learned of our presence, and many of them begged to join us.

The batistianos also knew we were in the cane country, but they didn't come after us. One night we tried to lure the two dozen soldiers and policemen in Cabañas into a trap. We set up an ambush less than a mile south of Cabañas, on the highway to Artemisa, and two men—Pipilo and El Puro, who had joined us in October—were sent into town. The two guerrillas, dressed as civilians, each carried an automatic pistol under his sport shirt. They shot out an electric transformer and peppered the front of the police station before trotting away down the Artemisa highway. Not long after Pipilo and El Puro rejoined us at our ambush position, it became clear that the batistianos were not going to take the bait. Our peasant friends reported that both the police and the Rural Guards had barricaded themselves inside their cuarteles.

The peasants were jubilant, for they were now convinced that the batistianos were afraid of the guerrillas. The projected ambush became a fiesta in the middle of the highway. Claudio persuaded a local storekeeper to open his establishment to sell us cold beer. We sat around on the pavement drinking beer with our peasant friends and talking loudly and boastfully. We knew that the soldiers stationed in Cabañas wouldn't crash our party, but we couldn't be sure of the larger garrisons at Artemisa and Bahía Honda. After an hour we broke off the celebration and departed for the sierra, leaving the highway littered with broken bottles so the enemy would know that we had had a good time.

We dominated all the sugar country at night. During

the daytime the batistianos controlled the area along the highways and north of them to the coast, but they ceded to us the cane fields at the foot of the mountains. The enemy learned that Titi and his family were aiding the guerrillas, but they couldn't make arrests because they were afraid to go near his home. Once we waited for the batistianos all day along the sugar mill railroad near Titi's house. Our friends in this area were safe, but the peasants who lived close to the highways were at the mercy of government forces. It was absolutely essential that we eliminate all informers from the area.

One suspected informer, a fairly prosperous colono who lived beside one of the Mercedita rail lines, knew he was in danger and had sent his family away. When the guerrillas arrived to search his house before dawn one morning, it was deserted. The man, a middle-aged Negro, was found sleeping in a tool shed in the yard. When told that he was going to be executed, he asked only for permission to urinate. After he finished and broke wind two or three times, he was hanged from one of his own shade trees. He must have thought it all a nightmare from which he would awake at any moment.

"He is no informer," Pipilo said to Alberto and me, speaking of the dead man in the present tense. "A batistiano, yes, but an informer, no." Nevertheless, Claudio had decided that a known Batista sympathizer should not live among our supporters. His body was cut down from the tree and hoisted twenty-five feet to the top of a concrete frame—a structure that straddled the tracks and supported the pulleys that, during the harvest season, lifted sugar cane onto railcars. Then we returned to our camp in the mountains. When the sun rose the dangling corpse could be seen from the nearby highway. Afraid to expose themselves to possible sniper fire, the police and Rural Guards refused to cut it down. Not until late afternoon did the batistiano mayor of Cabañas appear to remove his friend's body personally.

Claudio's band more than doubled in the month after the Las Pozas attack. "We need rifles for the new men," I told the captain, "and we need machine guns, and ammunition also." He agreed. "In the United States," I continued, "these things are easy to obtain. Over there one can also buy a thing for knocking down the walls of these cuarteles."

"A bazooka?" Claudio asked.

"A thing much better than that. It is a species of cannon called a recoilless rifle, caliber 57 millimeters. These cannons were used by the Army of the United States in Korea, but now the Army is selling them because they do not stop the new Russian tanks. But the tanks of Batista would be no problem. And one of these cannons could easily penetrate the walls of a cuartel. The cannon is light; it does not weigh much more than a bazooka. Claudio, what is so good about these things is their great range. We could put one of them on top of a hill two kilometers from the highway and—boom! whatever vehicle that appears, *se acaba.*"

"*¡Cojone'!*" The captain voiced his favorite exclamation, drawing out the second syllable and dropping the final *s*, as Cubans often do. "And you could buy one of these in the United States?"

"Yes, for only four or five hundred pesos—with plenty of ammunition. And good Springfield rifles for thirty pesos; Thompson *ametralladoras* for 150 pesos. Send me to the United States, Claudio, and I'll buy all these things for us and bring them in a boat to the beach over there. Then we could arm all the new men and have the most tremendous *guerrilla* this side of the Sierra Maestra."

"But you know that Escalona would be *muy bravo* if he learned that I let you go."

"Yes, but I would return. You have my word of honor."

The captain said he'd consider it, and I knew that he would. Claudio was not trying to put me off; he was not that kind of man. Besides, he was tired of running a boarding camp for refugees from the lowland. He wanted to give the newcomers weapons so they could be sent out to operate on their own.

Among the November recruits was a remarkable peasant from near Bahía Honda. A short, broad-shouldered, raw-boned man in his twenties, Juan Díaz was forceful, determined, ambitious, intelligent, and completely illiterate. He was a born leader. Before he was through, he would rise to the rank of captain in the Rebel Army, then lead a counterrevolutionary uprising, and finally die before a firing squad. Like Hubert Matos, Fidel's brilliant comandante in the Sierra Maestra, Juan Díaz came late to the guerrilla campaign. He tasted its victories without enduring the ordeal of the formative period. He and Matos would lose because they were unable to shatter the solidarity of the fidelista officer corps, which was founded not on the sharing of success, or even danger, but on the common experience of long months of hunger and fatigue in the sierra. Those who had remained with Fidel during this testing period were not likely to abandon him later.

Other newcomers to Claudio's band included Clemente —a personable mulatto who was a protégé of Miss Kerrigan, a Southern Baptist missionary in Cabañas—and a contingent of Methodists from Matanzas province. There were more Protestants in our group than practicing Catholics. Most of the men, however, were skeptics who made use of religion only in their oaths: God was a cuckold and a pile of shit and Jesus Christ was a queer, and they defecated on both of them and the Virgin, too. The theory that blasphemy is a sign of faith couldn't be proven in Cuba; the peasants and workers who used this language were true unbelievers. Few had received any religious training, because the dominant Catholic Church, like every other Cuban institution, ignored the rural masses. The peasants, however, did celebrate the religious holidays in December: Santa Barbara's Day, Saint Lazarus' Day, and Christmas Eve—*la noche buena*. These came near the beginning of the harvest season; the peasants who had survived the dead season could now buy food on credit. That was the real reason for the celebrations.

About 70 per cent of Claudio's men could read and write. That was somewhat below the Cuban national literacy rate, but far above the average for the small towns and rural areas from which most of them came. Although few had gone beyond elementary school, all had absorbed a great deal of Cuban history. They enjoyed telling me about the Cuban War for Independence and the march of the great mulatto general, Antonio Maceo, through Pinar del Río. Maceo occupied the town of Cabañas a few months before his death near Havana in 1896. Pipilo suggested that Maceo might have been killed not by the Spaniards but by his own white aide-de-camp. Pipilo said he didn't know if it were true or not, but "they say" that some whites in the liberation army conspired to kill the mulatto general so that after the war Cuba would not be ruled by an *hombre de color*. My comrades, like Cubans in general, delighted in repeating rumors and were devotees of conspiratorial interpretations of history.

Maceo seemed to provide the guerrillas with more inspiration than did José Martí, the intellectual leader of Cuba's independence movement. The fidelistas were adhering to a guerrilla tradition that originated in the wars of 1868–1898; they could identify with Maceo and other *mambí* heroes, like Negro General Quintín Bandera. Many tales were told about Bandera, who hated Spaniards both as a race and as individuals. It was said that Bandera's men had standing orders to bring all prisoners of war before him one at a time. The General would ask each captive his name—in Spanish, how he called himself. As soon as the prisoner replied, the black revolutionary, with a swish of his machete, would lop off the fellow's head. As he did so, Bandera would exclaim in the dialect of his people: *¡Sen yamaba!*—he *called* himself. The General's superiors in the liberation army were not amused; they were concerned about the bad effect his antics were having on foreign opinion. So he was ordered to stop shedding the blood of prisoners of war. Bandera duly acknowledged receipt of the order and then proceeded to do away with another hundred prisoners. When Generalísimo Máximo Gómez appeared and demanded an explanation, Bandera assured him that the order had been obeyed to the letter and not a drop of blood had been shed; all the prisoners had been hanged.

American intervention in 1898 thwarted the revolution that was the passionate vision of Bandera. The fidelistas in 1958 did not want to relive the experience of the mambises. "We want to be friends with the United States," said Ramoncito, the gardner from Havana, "but we don't want your government to send troops to our country—not even to overthrow Batista. We only want the good will of the American people—and the help of Americans like you. We are not communists; we are *anti*-communists." Ramoncito was sincere. Another time he said to me, "You have no idea what it means to have an American with us."

Americans were respected in Cuba, and as individuals they were liked. Philip Cooper, the manager of the Mercedita sugar mill, was considered a good person. Claudio and the other guerrillas from around Mercedita fondly remembered *Míster* Cooper's son, Philip-*cito*, who was a few years older than most of them. They would do nothing to hurt the Coopers, though they wouldn't hesitate to take away all the land of the Cuban-American Sugar Refining Company and give it to the peasants. But they would do the same with the holdings of the Cuban Casanova family at Orozco. Americans certainly were not considered the primary cause of Cuba's social ills in 1958. In eastern Pinar del Río only a small fraction of the land was owned by Americans, and the *yanqui* presence was far from overwhelming. Once I was introduced to a peasant in the sierra, who became excited and immediately went to fetch his wife, for she had never seen an americano.

All my comrades favored changes in Cuba's social and economic structure. They wanted land for all the peasants and year-round employment for everyone who desired it. They wanted to remove the tax burden from the poor; the Cuban peasant paid excise taxes on his shoes, on his work clothes, even on the matches he used to light his miserable charcoal stove. But the guerrillas had no idea how to bring about these changes; they would leave that up to Fidel. They weren't by any means firmly committed to the democratic process; everyone deprecated politicians and political rhetoric, and nobody expressed any burning desire to vote in an election, or run for office, or write an article in a newspaper.

In November it began to get chilly at night, especially during the early morning hours when we usually returned to camp after prowling in the lowlands. I began sleeping with three blankets, but even this was not enough to keep out the cold air that whisked around and under my cotton hammock. Several of the men sought warmth by sleeping on the ground, though they risked a soaking if it rained. A plastic cloth was stretched out on a rope that ran above and parallel to my hammock, which at least fairly well protected me from the rain. Except when there were strong winds, which was rare, the only water that could touch me were the few drops that trickled down the hammock ropes.

After the cold and the rain, mosquitoes gave us the most discomfort. They were no great problem when we slept, since they could not penetrate the thickness of the blankets in which we completely wrapped ourselves. They were most irritating to those on guard duty between sunrise and sunset. The only protection a poor sentry had was to put a blanket around his head and shoulders while keeping a cloud of cigar smoke in front of his face. One of the few improvements wrought by the flood of recruits in October and November was an increased guard roster; no longer did everyone have to serve a two-hour turn every other night. There were two men on each shift, with only the officers—Claudio and El Gallego—exempt from guard duty and hence safe from the mosquitoes. Next to man, the mosquito was the most venomous creature in Cuba; there were no poisonous snakes or insects.

We walked much greater distances in November than in any previous month, but we never knew exactly how much ground we covered. Not even Claudio had a map. Distances in the countryside were reckoned in leagues, roughly four miles, which was how far a horse was supposed to walk in an hour. Kilometers were used only for measuring highway distances. The peasants were unfamiliar with the official metric units and gave measurements either in the English system introduced by the American occupation in 1898 or in Spanish colonial terms. Whether we were treading *kilómetros, millas,* or *leguas,* we wore out many shoes in the process. I learned that any ill-fitting pair of shoes eventually would conform to the feet, or the feet would conform to the shoes. A new pair of shoes inevitably raised new blisters and brought about a shifting of callouses, but the process was finally not disabling. Our socks were of thin cotton and gave little cushioning; they were not always used.

Claudio had been operating independently for four weeks. He had received his last orders from Escalona in person on October 10. At that time the Comandante had said nothing about disrupting the elections of November 3. Since we had no short-wave receiver, we didn't hear Fidel on Radio Rebelde order all units to shoot candidates and burn ballot boxes. In the absence of these orders, we did not take part in the election campaign. It was in the two weeks following the voting that we brought the Mercedita-Orozco sugar country under our control during nighttime.

After dark the only show of enemy strength outside the towns was a regular highway patrol of two Military Intelligence Service (SIM) squad cars that were based in Guanajay. The radio-equipped Chevrolets escorted the last bus of the day from Artemisa to Bahía Honda, via Cabañas, and arrived at the end of the line at about 9:30. The bus remained at Bahía Honda overnight, but the cars returned to their base at Guanajay, checking in at Orozco on their way home. Although this particular patrol didn't stop along the highway to bother anyone, the SIM was reputed to be one of the most brutal agencies of the dictatorship. Claudio first made the decision to wipe out the patrol; then he brought up for discussion the matter of how best to do it.

The consensus held that we should attack the cars on the return trip, which would allow us to move from the sierra to our ambush positions under cover of darkness.

The trouble with the return-trip idea was that the batistianos were so afraid of an ambush and in such a hurry to get home that they travelled seventy to eighty miles per hour, maintaining a distance of one hundred to two hundred yards between cars. If the first vehicle was fired upon, or crashed into an obstacle, the second would be alerted in time to avoid the trap. It seemed impossible to set up simultaneous ambushes for the two cars, because the exact distance between them at any given place would not be known. The problem could be solved by finding a stretch of highway where the cars habitually slowed down and came close together. Claudio suggested a narrow steel-girdered bridge just south of the Orozco mill. That night, November 14, four of us went to reconnoiter the bridge.

Claudio, El Gallego, Pipilo, and I left camp at dusk and arrived at the bridge at ten o'clock. From beneath the bridge we watched the enemy cars roar across at 10:15, heading for Orozco. Fifteen minutes later they passed again, this time on their way back to the northern highway. They approached more slowly the second time—there was a slight dip in the pavement just north of the bridge—and the gap between them was shortened to less than one hundred yards. As the first car emerged from the bridge, the second was entering it.

It seemed to me that both cars could be trapped on the bridge, and I offered Claudio a plan. One tommy gun and our Star machine pistol would open up on the first car from behind the concrete pillars at the south end of the bridge as the vehicle approached the exit. At the same moment, the other Thompson and the San Cristóbal would fire on the rear of the second car just as it drove onto the bridge. Our shotgunners would help the automatic-weapons men seal off the ends of the bridge, while the riflemen, positioned in the creekbed below, would pour lead up into the cars and pick off any soldiers who might emerge and silhouette themselves against the moonlit sky.

Pipilo liked my plan, but El Gallego thought it too risky. Claudio agreed with his lieutenant. Even if both cars were disabled on the bridge, we couldn't hope to kill all the occupants in the first burst of fire. Some of the bastistianos would recover from the initial shock and shoot back. Finding themselves trapped, they would take desperate measures. They might rush one end of the bridge and overwhelm our men there; maybe some would even jump off the bridge with guns blazing and hit some of the riflemen in the creekbed. And with our men firing in three directions, somebody might be wounded or killed by friendly fire. We had lost Tite at Las Pozas and Serafín at Soroa; the captain didn't want any casualties this time.

The idea of attacking the cars on the return trip was dismissed altogether, so we now turned our thoughts to ambushing them as they accompanied the bus. The cars tried to follow the bus at a safe distance, but tended to close in on it when it labored uphill. The last stretch of the route, from the Orozco cutoff to Bahía Honda, was perfectly flat and offered no suitable ambush sites. The attack would have to be carried out about nine o'clock, or before the vehicles entered this stretch. This meant that we would have less than two hours of darkness to get into position. We would have to cross several miles of cane country before sundown, but since the peasants who lived in the area were our friends, Claudio was willing to risk the crossing. We would strike on the night of November 17.

Without further reconnaissance, Claudio chose for the ambush a site he knew well: a curve in the northern highway at the top of a fairly steep grade two miles west of Cabañas. Five of the new men, who were armed only with revolvers and .22 rifles, were detailed to maintain the camp and guard the prisoners. The remaining thirty-three guerrillas left for the highway at three o'clock in the afternoon. Four hours later we arrived at a point two hundred yards from the ambush site; there, in a cane field at the base of the ridge along which the highway ran, we waited for darkness.

As the last glow of the sun melted away on the horizon, Claudio, El Gallego, Mesa, Juan Díaz, and I left the others to survey the ambush site. From the cane field we ascended through a *marabú* thicket to the highway, crossed to the other side, and climbed to the top of a twenty-foot embankment. We looked over the ground as Claudio gave us our orders.

Juan Díaz was to requisition the jeep that was standing at a store a few yards over the hill. He would park it off the road, just around the curve toward Bahía Honda. Upon receiving word from the top of the embankment that the bus and the patrol cars had been sighted, Juan Díaz was to drive the jeep into the middle of the highway—but still around the curve, hidden from the view of the oncoming vehicles. There he would abandon the jeep and run for the ditch at the foot of the embankment. In the ditch he would join a party of five pistoleers commanded by Mesa. Their mission was to prevent the bus from resuming its journey once it stopped to avoid hitting the jeep.

The remainder of the guerrillas were to line the top of the embankment for thirty yards along the approach to the curve. They would be divided into two groups of about a dozen men each. I was to command one group, which would fire on the first car, while the other group, led by El Gallego, would shoot at the second car. Claudio would be located between the two groups and give the order to commence firing as soon as the first car passed him. He would add the automatic fire of his San Cristóbal to that of El Gallego's Thompson in shooting at the second car. Pipilo's Thompson and the Star—formerly Tite's and now assigned to Sergio, a newcomer—would be directed by me.

At 8:15 the men in the cane field were summoned to take up their ambush positions. I placed Pipilo and his tommy gun at the head of my line, closest to the curve, so that he could shoot obliquely into the first car's windshield. If the pile-up between the bus and the jeep didn't halt the patrol car, Pipilo would have to stop it. Next to Pipilo came Sergio and his Star. Sergio's weapon was terribly inaccurate, but it could throw a lot of lead in the general direction of the target and a few bullets were bound to hit it. Next in line came six shotgunners who, if all went well, would be closest to the car when the shooting started. At the end of my sector I put four riflemen. I placed myself at the center, between two shotgunners. El Gallego's portion of the line was similarly constituted— with riflemen on the far end and shotgunners between them and the automatic weapons.

After the men were in position, I suggested to Claudio

that two or three shotgunners be detached and positioned across the highway, down the bank in the marabú thicket. There they would be in defilade, and hence in no danger of being hit by friendly fire from above. From there, too, they could shoot down any soldiers who might escape from the cars and seek refuge in the brush.

Claudio rejected the suggestion. To engage the enemy at night in a marabú thicket, he felt, would cause confusion and invite trouble. It would be wiser to concede the thicket to any batistianos who might escape from the cars. Since these men would be wounded and therefore desperate, any attempt to halt their escape or flush them from their hiding places would be met with last-ditch resistance which would surely cost us some casualties. All the guerrillas, Claudio decided, would remain in position on the north side of the highway until all the soldiers had been killed or driven from the cars. We would not venture into the thicket.

Only one vehicle passed the ambush site between seven and nine o'clock. It was a late-model Ford that came screeching into the curve at about seventy miles per hour from the direction of Bahía Honda. As the car roared past, El Gallego recognized it as belonging to the mayor of Cabañas. The mayor, who was riding in the back seat, knew he was marked for assassination. He escaped death that night only because we were stalking bigger game.

At exactly nine o'clock a flash of headlights appeared on the eastern horizon. *¡Viene la guagua!*—the bus is coming—someone shouted. There was a quick chorus of metallic clacking as weapons were cocked and cartridges fed into the chambers. It was a bright night, with a half-moon hanging in the western sky, and the bus came into full view as it crossed the horizon, about three hundred yards away. Right behind it came the two patrol cars. They followed the bus down a slight incline and fell in close behind as it chugged up the grade toward the curve.

As the bus rounded the curve at the top of the hill, its headlights fell upon the jeep in the middle of the road. The bus rumbled to a stop, and the first car rolled up to within ten yards of it and halted, perfectly centered in front of my guns. At that moment Claudio opened up on the second car, now fifteen yards behind the first and squarely in front of El Gallego's men. Immediately guerrilla fire began pouring in on the cars from all along the line.

Then things seemed to go wrong. The bus got away. After briefly pausing in front of the jeep, the bus driver gunned his motor and snaked to the left around the obstacle. Mesa's pistoleers vainly fired at his tires. Claudio wanted Mesa to hold the driver and passengers until we withdrew. There were usually dependents of Bahía Honda-based soldiers on the bus, and they would come in handy as hostages should Captain Iturriaga decide to pursue us.

Those of us who were firing at the patrol cars, however, gave little thought to the bus's escape. We were primarily concerned with the occupants of the cars, who seemed to persist in shooting back at us. In less than two minutes the cars had been riddled by hundreds of rifle and submachine gun slugs; countless loads of buckshot had crashed through the windows. Nevertheless we could still see the muzzle flashes of return fire, so we continued to send round after round smashing into the enemy vehicles. I couldn't understand how there could be anyone still alive in those cars.

Claudio quickly realized that his men were firing at the

strikes of their own bullets. The "muzzle flashes" were sparks produced by the impact of guerrilla bullets against the steel frames of the cars. The captain had to shout "Cease fire!" three times before everybody got the word. Then the night became very quiet, the way it had been two minutes before. The only sound was a low hum emanating from the motionless vehicles; the engines of both cars were still running.

The captain scrambled down the embankment, glanced about, then ordered his men to follow. Guerrillas milled around the cars, talking loudly and gesticulating wildly. Some pointed excitedly at the two corpses sprawled on the highway. Pipilo spotted a third body lying just inside the thicket. When Pipilo announced that he was going to blast it with his Thompson, the body rose and walked forward with hands in the air.

While Pipilo was interrogating his prisoner, Claudio was chewing out Mesa for allowing the bus to get away. Instead of staying in the ditch, Mesa and his men should have boarded the bus when it stopped. Now we would have to work rapidly to search and destroy the cars and get out of the area before the Rural Guards from Bahía Honda could get there. We all believed that Iturriaga would make an attempt to rescue his ambushed comrades. I was inspecting the first car when Claudio shouted at me to take Pipilo, Sergio, and a couple of riflemen and set up an outpost just over the hill to stop anyone coming from Bahía Honda.

I gathered together the riflemen and Star-gunner Sergio and approached Pipilo who was still occupied with the prisoner, a first lieutenant. As a member of SIM the officer was, *ipso facto*, a "war criminal." El Puro, holding a flashlight in his teeth, went through the prisoner's wallet. He extracted the lieutenant's SIM identification card and handed it to Pipilo. Confronted with the evidence, the officer denied that he was responsible for any crimes and described himself as "simply a military man who carries out orders." Pipilo dispatched him with a single shot from his tommy gun. Then he walked away with me to set up the outpost over the hill.

After sending another party two hundred yards down the road to guard the Cabañas approach, Claudio directed the searching of the cars. The guerrillas found no more enemy dead inside. The front and rear doors on the left side of both cars were open. The right front door of the first car was also open; the batistiano who had tried to take this exit was lying on the pavement with his left foot still inside the door. The man's weapon, a Springfield rifle, was found in the car. Another Springfield was discovered with its stock split near the body of a soldier who had emerged from the left side of the second car. Except for a .45 automatic pistol taken from the lieutenant, no other weapons were captured.

The ammunition yield wasn't quite so disappointing. There were about three hundred rifle cartridges in the dead soldiers' bandoliers. A pouch of five San Cristóbal magazines loaded with twenty rounds each and about two hundred more carbine cartridges in boxes were also found. Only a handful of .45 pistol cartridges were discovered.

El Gallego began saying that it was time to get out of there. At 9:15 Claudio ordered him to gather up all the men who were standing idly by the cars and take them down the highway and around the thicket to the cane field. The captain and Quintín stayed behind to douse the upholstery of the cars with gasoline, which they caught in canteen cups as it flowed from bullet holes in the gas tanks. This done, Claudio called in my outpost. We arrived in time to help drag the enemy bodies off the highway. Then we stepped off briskly down the road as the captain and Quintín tossed burning rags into the cars and under their leaky gas tanks.

Great yellow flames were leaping skyward as Claudio and Quintín overtook us about fifty yards down the highway. As we paused briefly to watch the fires, the captain summoned the eastern outpost to join us. More than $6,000 worth of government property was going up in smoke: two brand-new 1959 Chevrolet sedans with automatic transmissions and air conditioning. But we couldn't afford to stand there gawking for long. It was 9:30 and enemy troops might already be on their way to the scene. We veered off the highway and followed a path into the cane field where we joined El Gallego and the rest of the band.

The reunion came none too soon for El Gallego. It was time to head for the hills, he told Claudio. Just then the sound of gunfire erupted from the highway. *¡Los soldados!* somebody gasped. A few men seemed on the verge of panic.

"Those are not shots!" Claudio shouted. "Look, they are bullets exploding in the fire." The leaping yellow flames had subsided and a steady orange glow surrounded the frames of the cars. The "shots" came from the second car, where dancing white flashes could be seen against the orange background.

"We should have found those bullets," I said to El Gallego. "Instead of worrying so much about getting home, we should have been gathering the fruits of victory."

El Gallego roared with laughter. "Gathering the fruits of victory! What a beautiful phrase! El Americano really came up with a gem that time. He should be a poet." The whole band joined in the good-natured laughter as tension rapidly subsided. The return march was orderly, and we arrived at our camp at 2:30 on the morning of November 18.

5 CLAUDIO DECIDED TO LET ME GO TO
the United States to arrange an arms deal. I had to get out
of Cuba before November 28 because my tourist card was
only good for ninety days at a time. If I tried to leave the
country after that, the police would arrest me when I presented my papers at the Havana airport. On the morning
after the highway ambush Claudio said that I could leave
for Havana the next day, which was November 19. We
agreed that I would return to Titi's house on the night
of December 1. The captain gave me 100 pesos for the
trip, instructing me to bring back a list of firm prices and,
if possible, photographs of the weapons that I had arranged to buy. If I kept the deal under $10,000, including
transportation, it could be consummated quickly, for there
would be little delay in raising the money.

Passports were not required for travel between the
United States and Cuba so I gave mine to Claudio, with
the understanding that he would send it to the American
embassy in Havana if I failed to return. The following
note was to be delivered to the embassy with the passport:

A la Embajada de los E.U.A., La Habana:
There are four copies of this message: no. one will be
carried on my person; no. two will be dispatched with
my passport (#32235 USA) to the U.S. Embassy in

Havana in the event that I do not reach my destination; no. three in this event will be dispatched to Senator Wayne Morse, a Champion of Liberty in the USA; and the last will go to the United Press International.

I demand that my rights under international law as a foreign national in Cuba be respected; that I be afforded the same treatment before Cuban Justice as is entitled a citizen of this nation. However, everyone should know that there is no justice nor respect for law or for the rights of anyone in Cuba under the Batista dictatorship. Batista's "police" are sadistic murderers who are attempting to crush the free spirit of the Cuban people under a reign of terror. They cannot succeed. If I am tortured, mutilated, or murdered, it is my desire that such facts be made known to the world, and especially to the USA, which has too often aided even the most odious dictatorships.

I request that my disappearance in Cuba be investigated.

I signed all four copies and made a Spanish translation for Claudio. The copies for the embassy, Senator Morse, and the UPI were in English and remained with Claudio. I carried the one in Spanish. This scheme, which I thought up, was supposed not only to give me some protection from the batistianos but also to assure Claudio that I wouldn't desert; I led him to believe that I would be in big trouble in *los Estado Unidos* if the authorities learned that I had been serving with the fidelistas. It was not until he had seen these notes that he set a date for my departure.

On the morning of November 19 El Indio gave me a haircut and shaved off my beard except for the moustache, which he trimmed. Local peasants contributed go-to-town clothing: draped and pegged pin-striped pants, pointed-toed shoes, and the typical Cuban frilly white shirt, called a *guayabera.* "You look like a real *chulo* now," Pipilo remarked when I was all decked out. After lunch I waved goodbye to everyone, reminding them that I'd see them again in two weeks, and left with a peasant guide. Neither of us was armed.

We walked south and east, away from the cane country, through an abandoned coffee plantation. There were still some coffee trees growing on the cool slopes under the shade of larger trees where peasants came several times a year to pick the beans. The plantation's drying deck and the massive stone foundations of several buildings, covered with vines and strangler figs, looked like some pre-Columbian ruin perched on the side of the mountain next to a little waterfall. I thought I'd like to buy that place after the Revolution and become a coffee planter.

We arrived at the edge of a rolling pasture, where my guide pointed to a trail which, he said, led to the Cabañas-Artemisa highway some fifteen minutes away. There I could flag down the bus to Artemisa which was due to pass in about half an hour. In Artemisa I could catch a bus to Havana. I said goodbye to the guide and began walking down the trail through the pasture; it was three o'clock and the sun was very hot. A modest house stood at the junction of the trail and the highway. A man and a boy were outside. I greeted them and asked if the bus had passed. No, not yet, they said, but it should arrive any minute.

From my speech the man must surely have known that I was a foreigner. He probably guessed that I was El Americano of *la guerrilla* of Captain Claudio. For all I knew, he might have been an informer, but I couldn't avoid speaking to him. Anyway, I thought, my reputation, which had been greatly inflated in the rumors that the peasants liked to bounce around, would probably deter him from turning me in. I decided to display great confidence, as if I knew the whole fidelista army was lurking over the ridge behind us and watching our every move. I remarked on how hot it was, and asked the fellow for a glass of water, which his son promptly brought to me. I drained the glass and patted the boy on the head as I handed it back. I thanked them both profusely and called out a hearty *¡adiós!* when the bus appeared a few moments later.

At my signal the bus stopped. I jumped aboard with the exact fare in my hand. There were quite a few people on the bus, but I found an unoccupied double seat and slumped in next to the window. Half a mile down the road an army corporal got on and sat down beside me. Rural Cubans are a talkative bunch, and I knew that if the corporal tried to strike up a conversation with me I would be in trouble. Fortunately he began speaking with a woman he recognized across the aisle. If he turned to me, I decided not to try to conceal the fact that I was an American; I'd say that I was visiting Miss Kerrigan, the Baptist missionary in Cabañas. But the occasion didn't arise, and I was greatly relieved when the corporal left the bus a few miles down the road at Cayajabos.

I got off at the end of the line in Artemisa and immediately boarded a bus for Havana that was waiting at the station. Just before the bus pulled out, a woman sat down beside me. She kept up a steady stream of chatter as we rolled on toward Guanajay. I kept gazing out the window, only nodding or mumbling *sí* when I thought it absolutely necessary. Finally, in exasperation, the lady turned to the woman seated behind her and said, "I think he is a *bobo*"— a moron. She didn't bother me for the rest of the trip.

The first thing I bought when I reached Havana was a canvas grip bag. Then I purchased a pair of Cuban-style cowboy pants and some loafers and put away the scruffy pointed-toe shoes and threadbare pegged pants and assumed the role of an American tourist in native costume. I got a two-peso room in the Gran Hotel near Central Park and had supper at a Chinese lunch counter where the employees were nice about giving returning American tourists their change in American dollars. The next morning I checked in at the *Aerovías Q* office at the foot of the Prado, where I got a reservation for that afternoon's flight to Key West. There were no problems at the airport, though all carry-on bags were searched and all boarding males were frisked for guns. The officials apologetically explained that some of their aircraft had recently been hijacked.

The plane arrived in Key West in time for me to clear customs and immediately board a Greyhound for Miami. I didn't call my wife until the bus made a dinner stop at Marathon Key. Thanksgiving vacation was coming up, and she was to meet me on Wednesday night, November 26, in Atlanta. That gave me six days to devote full time to the search for arms.

I found what I wanted in an upper-middle-class neighborhood of a Southern city. There were American machine guns, recoilless rifles, and bazookas; Swedish automatic rifles; German and American submachine guns; hand grenades, ammunition, plastic explosives—all this collected by a college boy and stored in the basement of his parents' home. His prices were reasonable and he said that the items I wanted that were not on hand—another Thompson submachine gun and twenty Springfield rifles—could be gotten in a matter of days. He added that he could have all the stuff delivered anywhere in Virginia, Georgia, or the Carolinas, but that he'd rather stay clear of Florida. That was fine with me, since I was thinking of shipping the stuff from the Carolina coast. I took pictures of his arsenal and for $5 bought two carbine conversion kits to take back with me to Cuba that would convert our semiautomatic carbines to full automatics. I told my supplier that he would hear from me in about a month.

After my wife came south from the University of Michigan, we spent a few days with my parents. She was three and a half months pregnant and our marriage was no longer a secret. My wife accompanied me on a trip to the coast, where I located a shrimp boat captain who agreed to take the arms to Cuba for $2,000. The whole deal—delivery in Pinar del Río of enough weapons to arm thirty men—would come to less than five grand. I promised my wife that I would quit the Revolution as soon as I had delivered the guns. On Sunday, November 30, she returned to Ann Arbor, and the next day I took a plane from Charleston to Jacksonville, where I made connections for Miami and Havana. This time I brought my camera to Cuba.

When I went through customs in Havana, the carbine conversion kits—each consisting of eight tiny pieces and a lever about four inches long—were taped to the inside of my thighs. The photographs of the arms and the protective letter were in my socks under the arches of my feet. Wedged between the pictures were some dynamite caps and firecracker fuses. I had run some tests in South Carolina and found that the fuse of a cherry bomb would set off a dynamite cap; with these caps and short fuses we could make throwable bombs out of the dynamite we had in the sierra. I had no trouble bringing this contraband through customs. They could have stripped me to shorts and socks and still not found it, but, as it turned out, incoming passengers were not even frisked.

It was after nine o'clock when I arrived in Havana. Too late, I decided, to try to get to the hills that night. Claudio, I knew, would wait three or four more days before sending my passport to the embassy, so I wasn't worried about arriving a little behind schedule. I checked in at the Gran Hotel with the idea of visiting Manolo the next day, whom I would ask to get a taxi to take me to Pinar del Río. On the morning of December 2 I rang the bell at my friend's apartment. The woman who came to the door said she had never heard of Manolo. I knew then that the police had gotten him, and sensed that I'd better get the hell out of the area; this lady was probably going to call the cops as soon as I left. I sought refuge in the bar of the Hotel Nacional.

In air-conditioned comfort I sipped a beer while planning my next moves. I decided to check out of the Gran Hotel that afternoon and catch a bus for Artemisa, where I'd take the last bus to Cabañas. I would get off just south of town, where we drank beer on the highway, and walk from there to Titi's house. This time I would travel as an American tourist, wearing a light grey suit, a blue sports shirt, and loafers and carrying a grip bag and camera. I had already shaved off my moustache. I'd pretend to be on my way to visit Miss Kerrigan and would speak no

Spanish. If anyone on the bus spoke English and asked why I was getting off south of town, I'd say that I thought that was where Miss Kerrigan lived. I might have to let somebody escort me to the missionary's house, but I could sneak out later in the night.

I ordered another beer and surveyed the dimly lit room. A couple of bar stools away an American tourist and a fat Cuban were carrying on a conversation in English. The Cuban, who was wearing a guayabera, paid for their drinks with a Diners' Club card. "I'll admit this is a dictatorship," he said to his drinking companion, "but what can you expect of us Cubans? Look at our mother country, Spain. Franco runs Spain. Batista's not nearly as bad as Franco. You Americans are lucky. You're descended from the English. England has the most stable democracy in the world."

There seemed to be no shortage of American tourists at the Hotel Nacional, although the manager, Thomas Kelley, had told a *Wall Street Journal* reporter the month before that his business was down 50 per cent because of the Revolution. If the underground was really doing its job, I thought, there wouldn't be a single tourist in Havana. Terrorist activity in the city had fallen off since the April general strike, yet noise or stink bombs were still occasionally set off in department stores or movie theaters. Unlike their counterparts in Algiers and Saigon, Havana terrorists couldn't bring themselves to toss hand grenades into crowded restaurants. But the Cuban who exploded a harmless petard and was caught could expect no more mercy from the batistianos than an Algerian terrorist captured by the *paras*. Those who were killed on the spot were the lucky ones; the others were taken to police dungeons where they were worked over by accomplished sadists before being put out of their misery. The only ones spared were those who had family connections high in Batista's government and somehow managed to alert their relatives before it was too late. The people who set off these nuisance bombs were for the most part students. They knew how to die, if not how to kill.

It was obvious that Batista had the situation in Havana well under control in early December. The students and the middle-class resistance leaders had long since given up hope for an urban uprising and had decided to back the fidelista guerrilla campaign. It was a decision they would soon regret. The guerrillas would indeed strangle the dictatorship, but the elimination of Batista on New Year's Day would remove the only real basis for collaboration between the liberal democrats of the cities and the social revolutionaries of the countryside. When the showdown came, the idealistic and faction-ridden liberals would be no match for the ruthless and disciplined peasant army which their money had helped create.

While I was in the United States I had learned of fidelista progress in the provinces east of Pinar del Río. American radio newscasts occasionally carried items on rebel activity in Oriente and Las Villas, or mentioned that Batista was court-martialing some officers for failure to fight. In Cuba I was sometimes able to pick up WGBS in Miami on Claudio's AM transistor, but while in the United States I listened to a newscast almost every hour. I also read the *Miami Herald* and *Time* magazine. The latter, in its issue of December 1, carried a map that showed most of Oriente and much of Camagüey and Las Villas under rebel control. The fact that the sierras of Pinar del Río were represented as an "operating area" indicated that *Time* was conservative in its estimate of fidelista strength; I would have colored the *pinareña* mountains red to show rebel control. I clipped out the map; when it was time to catch the bus to Artemisa, I put it in my shoe along with the photos and the dynamite caps.

I arrived in Artemisa at 4:30, an hour before the departure of the Cabañas bus, and settled in at a sidewalk café, where I sipped beer and gawked at the natives. I waved to everyone who stared back at me. A boy shined my shoes. Using sign language and repeating the name Cabañas, I got him to lead me to the bus, for which I gave him an American-sized tip. Smiling at everyone on the bus, I chose a left window seat near the front.

The trip took less than an hour, but, the sky being overcast, it was already quite dark as the bus approached Cabañas. I had difficulty making out the roadside terrain. A large bank appeared on the left. This was the place of our earlier party in the middle of the highway. I jumped up and shouted *¡Aquí! ¡Aquí!* The driver slowed down but pointed ahead, saying, "Cabañas." I could see the lights of the town just down the road.

¡Aquí! ¡Aquí! I insisted, and the driver finally stopped. Several passengers smiled and shook their fingers, giving the Cuban sign for *no* as I got off. Rapidly I strode down the highway away from the bus, stepping down hard on the dynamite caps in my shoes. In a minute I was in the cut where we had hoped to ambush the Cabañas soldiers; a minute later I found the trail that led through the cane fields to the rail line that went by Titi's house. Breathing

hard, I veered off the pavement onto the trail. Once clear of the highway I stopped to remove the conversion kits from my thighs and to take the dynamite caps and other things from my loafers and put them in my pockets. I was standing in two inches of mud. The dry season was late in arriving that year, and the rains would continue through the middle of December.

It didn't rain on the night of December 2, but every-thing was wet from earlier rains. Clouds hung low in the sky, blacking out all light and masking the features of the terrain. The trail, which frequently mingled with other paths, was impossible to follow. Two weeks under the artificial lights of Havana and the United States had ruined my night vision. Once again the dark, the guerrilla's friend and protector, was my enemy.

I lost my loafers in the mud shortly after I left the highway. Barefooted I stumbled and slid along what I took to be the trail. Soon I was lost in a maze of sugar cane. The fields were flooded, and when I stepped off into a drainage ditch I found myself in water up to my neck. My greatest concern was for my Ricohflex camera which, like everything else I carried, was completely submerged. I struggled out of the ditch and staggered on, oblivious of the briers that were piercing my feet. Then my toes touched the smooth surface of an iron rail, jolting me from my stupor. Although the tracks were under twelve inches of water, I was able to follow them by running one foot on top of the rail. When the tracks emerged from the slough and started up a steep grade, I knew I was heading in the right direction. This was the way Juan had brought me three months before.

It was nearly two o'clock in the morning when I arrived

at Titi's house. After I gave the fidelista bird call, Titi and his father greeted me warmly and provided me with hot coffee and dry clothing. Titi's father was sorry he couldn't offer me a cigar, but in my coat pocket I found a soggy butt which I finally managed to light and smoke down to the last shreds of tobacco, much to the old man's amusement. When Titi told me that Claudio had waited for me at the house throughout the previous night, I deeply regretted not making the effort to arrive on time. My comrades probably thought I had run out on them.

The next afternoon Titi led me to the rebel camp. The first guerrillas I embraced were the sentries: San Antonio and Padrón, the son of the mayor of Candelaria. Padrón was carrying his long-barreled Luger. The prisoners were now members of our band.

6 WHILE I WAS IN THE UNITED STATES
a messenger from Escalona's headquarters brought Claudio
orders to lay low. It seems that the Comandante was disturbed by reports of our activity on the highway and
feared that we might get wiped out. Claudio was not to
initiate any more action; moreover, he had to get Escalona's
approval before moving his camp. A regular courier service
began operating between our band and the Comandante's
headquarters fifty miles to the west.

Escalona had orders from the Sierra Maestra to prepare
to receive Rebel Column Number Two, which had left
Oriente in September and was on its way to Pinar del Río.
This outfit consisted of ninety men commanded by Camilo
Cienfuegos; it was also called the Antonio Maceo Column,
since its mission was to duplicate the mulatto general's epic
march from Oriente to Pinar del Río during the War for
Independence. Our band was the easternmost of Escalona's
units, so we were to welcome the Maceo Column to the
province. Claudio's guerrillas spent the last week of November and the entire month of December waiting for
Camilo—although at the time we didn't know that this was
the reason for our inactivity. Perhaps Claudio knew, but
the rest of us only knew that Escalona had ordered him
to cease offensive operations.

Claudio seemed impressed by the photographs I brought him. Eager to close the arms deal, he decided to send a man into Havana to hunt up the money. For this mission he chose a man named Carlos, one of several recruits who had arrived while I was away. Carlos had more schooling than any other Cuban in the band; he had studied engineering for three years at the University, was the only Cuban guerrilla in Pinar del Río who spoke English, and obviously knew his way around the Havana underground.

A few days later, when it was time to send Chicho on the regular run to Escalona's headquarters, Claudio mentioned in his report that the americano had arranged for an arms shipment. He added that there were some pictures of the weapons but that he couldn't send them to his superior because "I do not have them." Claudio seldom went into unnecessary detail. He did ask the Comandante if he had any suggestions on how to finance the shipment.

Escalona's reply came the next week. Yes, the Comandante wrote, it was necesary to get more weapons. He explained that he was expecting an arms shipment into his area shortly, and that all his available funds were tied up in the deal. It would be *muy bueno* if Claudio could arrange a similar transaction, but he would have to find the money on his own. Escalona authorized Claudio to accept contributions from anyone "except the Communists."

Fidelistas had little difficulty raising money during the last months of the guerrilla struggle. With cash they had no trouble buying war matériel in the United States. Their biggest problem was getting the arms from the United States into the hands of the guerrillas in Cuba. U.S. customs agents seized several boatloads of weapons and ammunition in American waters, and Batista's planes and patrol boats maintained a constant surveillance of the Cuban coasts. The fidelistas in eastern Cuba largely solved their munitions problems by constructing air fields in rebel-held territory. Much more easily than boats, aircraft could evade American and Cuban authorities. According to the *Time* magazine map I showed Claudio, at the end of November there were five rebel landing strips in Oriente province and one in Camagüey.

Fidel's first planeload of arms had arrived in March, but it was not until July, when the fidelistas had turned back Batista's offensive, that air traffic into the Sierra Maestra became routine. At the beginning of the enemy offensive, in May, the rebels fielded only three hundred well-armed guerrillas. By July enough weapons had been captured or were being airlifted to the rebels to arm hundreds of peasants in Oriente. By October all of Oriente province, except the cities and larger towns, was under rebel control, and fidelista columns were pushing across Camagüey into Las Villas. Our situation in Pinar del Río in December was like that of the rebels in Oriente nine months earlier. There were hundreds of peasants who were eager to join our ranks, but we had no weapons for them and so had to refuse their offers to enlist as guerrillas. A high proportion of the men who were accepted into the guerrilla bands were inadequately armed; of more than two hundred guerrillas in Pinar del Río in December, fewer than fifty had military rifles, carbines, or submachine guns. The rest were *escopeteros*—shotgunners, or men armed only with pistols or .22 rifles. If we could bring in enough military weapons to arm the escopeteros and some of the peasant militia, we would have little trouble in wresting most of the province away from the nine hundred batistianos of the 6th Rural Guard Regiment.

Escalona was planning to import munitions by air, but Claudio agreed to my plan for a seaborne delivery. By leaving from the Carolina coast and steering clear of Florida, and by using a shrimp boat rather than one of the pleasure crafts that gun runners usually chartered, I had hoped to avoid detection by American authorities. There would be little to fear from the Cuban Coast Guard, since the boat would not approach the shore of Pinar del Río—from the direction of Key West, 140 miles away—until well after dark; the arms could thus be unloaded in Cabañas Bay and the vessel halfway back across the Florida Strait by sunrise. I told Claudio that for personal reasons I wanted to return to the United States with the shrimp boat. He agreed to let me go. All I could do now was wait for Carlos to return from Havana with the money.

Meanwhile I learned how the batistianos has reacted to our highway ambush. Claudio said that there had been four men in each car. The five men who escaped were badly wounded but managed to crawl into the marabú thicket, where they waited to be rescued. But the twelve Rural Guards at Cabañas had no intention of venturing from their cuartel that night. Captain Iturriaga wouldn't move his thirty soldiers out of Bahía Honda until he had assurances that a seventy-man force from Guanajay and Artemisa would converge on the ambush site. The first government troops arrived on the scene about six hours after the shooting. The delay probably cost the lives of four of the five wounded soldiers. Only one of the eight victims of the ambush survived.

Early on the night after the attack, Captain Iturriaga retaliated in what had come to be typical batistiano fashion: he seized fourteen peasants from their homes along the highway and hanged them. The victims were fidelista sympathizers, but none had participated in the planning or execution of the attack.

The punishment the batistianos meted out to peasants who were vaguely suspected of revolutionary activity contrasted sharply to the handling of known resistance leaders from the upper classes—*doctores* like José Miró Cardona and Felipe Pazos—who were long tolerated by the dictatorship before finally being forced into exile. The peasants couldn't flee abroad to safety; their only refuge was in the hills with the guerrillas. Those fidelistas in the sierras who were not themselves peasants soon adopted the peasant outlook on life, which was shaped by the treatment the peasantry traditionally received from the nation's governors. Cuban governments had never been much concerned about the peasant's right to live. In times of insurrection, the peasant was strung up on the whim of some officer; in peacetime, he was evicted from his land and left to starve in a wretched hovel, where his children would writhe in agony as they were slowly consumed by the parasitic worms in their bellies which went unattended by any doctor. The peasants thus had little compassion for their enemies and no use whatsoever for legal niceties. Although the destitute Cuban peasantry comprised less than 30 per cent of the population, they counted for much more because, unlike the bourgeoisie and the urban proletariat, they weren't distracted by ideological disputations. The peasants belonged to Fidel without qualm or qualification; they were the sword of the Revolution.

Before leaving for Havana in November I had given my M-1 carbine to Quintín, the little Negro from Havana. His original weapon, a Spanish Mauser carbine left over from the War for Independence, had been rendered useless when he shot up the last of his seven-millimeter ammunition at the SIM patrol cars. When I returned from the United States I assured my comrade that the M-1 carbine was still his, as I would be leaving again shortly and wouldn't be taking part in any more action. Furthermore, I had brought Quintín a present from the United States: some pieces that would convert his carbine to full automatic. Quintín watched with eager anticipation as I installed the conversion kit. When I had completed the job, Claudio allowed me to test fire it into the ground. I pushed the selector forward and squeezed off a burst of three rounds. Quintín jumped up and down with excitement; when I handed him the weapon, he embraced me. He caressed the carbine on whose wooden stock I had carved the word *Libertad* along with my wife's name, Nancy, and then proudly slung it over his shoulder and pointed to a pot of coffee and asked *¿Monsieur, quiere café-rú?*

Quintín invariably used this polyglot to offer me coffee. It began when we first met in September and he told me he was from Haiti. He had made the claim before, but none of the guerrillas believed him. To them he was just another Havana Negro.

Parlez-vous français? I asked.

Sí, sí. Francés, he answered, chuckling as the others looked on in wonderment.

Comment allez-vous, monsieur?

Cómo tale bú, monsieur? he repeated, grinning.

Voulez-vous un peu de café?

Sí, sí. Bule bú café-rú. In triumph he walked over and poured two cups. Thereafter I was *monsieur* and coffee was *café-rú.*

In December we drank a lot of coffee—boiled in an open pot on a kerosene stove and strained through a sock—while we sat around talking, playing cards, or reading magazines. Claudio's band continued to grow. Mundo, brother of Tite, the mulatto who was wounded at Las Pozas, joined us; he said Tite was safely hidden in Cabañas and making a good recovery. There was almost daily traffic between our camp and the town of Cabañas; supplies were brought in and stockpiled, messages were received and dispatched. Shortly after I returned from the U.S., Claudio sent my waterlogged camera to town to be repaired. I had it back in about a week, and for several days I amused myself and my comrades by taking pictures.

As the wait for Carlos entered its third week, I became moody and withdrew to myself. Some days I slept fourteen hours. The rains, which continued past the middle of the month and sometimes lasted all day, deepened my depression. We lived on a sea of mud and refuse. Our campsite, to which we had moved a few days after my return, was on a hill surrounded by ever expanding concentric rings of excrement. The nearly constant rain kept flies away and gradually washed the feces downhill. When going out, one never knew if he was stepping in mud or shit.

Miraculously, nobody got sick. Apparently only I was disturbed by the rain and the inactivity; my comrades were not. They were not at one another's throat, nor was there any noticeable increase in grumpiness among them. Boredom didn't bother them; they were content to lie about, smoke cigars, and, in many cases, eat regularly and well for the first time in their lives.

There was a bad accident during this period but it could have happened any time. A shotgun that a guerrilla was cleaning went off and tore into another man's shoulder. One of the men from Matanzas was immediately sent to fetch a doctor. Within twenty-four hours the guerrilla returned with the doctor and his equipment. Our wounded comrade—one of the November recruits, a boy of about twenty years old—was placed on an operating table made of hammocks stretched across a wooden frame; there the doctor removed the buckshot, cleaned the wound, and gave a blood transfusion. The doctor remained with us, and the patient seemed to respond to his treatment. About ten days after the accident, however, the boy died of gangrene.

Several times in December Claudio sent two or three guerrillas out to apprehend suspected informers. Claudio had some trouble deciding whether one prisoner, whom Alberto had brought in, was truly an informer. Alberto didn't know: Claudio had ordered him to arrest the man and he had done as he was ordered. After conferring with various local peasants, Claudio decided that the accused was guilty and early one morning had him hanged. As usual there was no trial, no ceremony. When I awoke, I was told that the prisoner was hanging from a tree in the woods. I grabbed my camera and went off to record the scene. When Claudio saw me he shook his finger, signaling "no pictures." I chose not to defy him.

Another suspect brought to our camp was a blond young man, the son of a colono. On his second night as a prisoner, my regular two-hour turn at guard duty came up.

Since I no longer had a weapon of my own, I borrowed Claudio's San Cristóbal automatic carbine. At two o'clock I relieved Pancho. Wrapped in a couple of blankets, I sat down a few feet from the prisoner, the gun across my knees. The prisoner was huddled under a plastic rain cover and, according to Pancho, his hands were bound and his shoeless feet were securely tied to the tree he was leaning against. He moaned and tossed about a little under the plastic sheet, which I considered normal for anyone trying to sleep in his situation. Suddenly he jumped up and made a run for it.

¡Alto! ¡Alto! I shouted as I got to my feet and brought the carbine to my shoulder. Sighting his white socks as he ran, I aimed at them and pressed the single-shot trigger four times. After the last shot, he lay on the ground about sixty feet from me, screaming in pain. Within seconds every guerrilla in camp was on the scene. All security regulations were forgotten; the men talked loudly and excitedly and used their flashlights indiscriminately.

¡Coño! Pipilo exclaimed as he examined the wounded prisoner. "The americano put three bullets in his leg! It is almost cut in two!"

"I was not trying to escape," the victim moaned. "He wanted to kill me."

"You eat shit," Pipilo snapped. "If you were not trying to escape, how did you get over here?" The bystanders laughed joyfully; they hugged me and slapped me on the back.

"He thought the americano was a bobo because he cannot speak Castilian well," El Indio observed with great delight.

"This is the bobo," Pipilo added, gesturing at the fallen

prisoner. "*¡Que estúpido!* Did you not know that the American is a veteran of the War of Korea and has an aim that never fails?"

Claudio was equally impressed. After he congratulated me, I asked to be excused from the remainder of my guard tour. Claudio assented, and I went to my hammock. My feelings were a mixture of disgust and elation. They hanged the prisoner that night; he was buried before I awoke the next morning.

I was afraid that Carlos had been captured by the police in Havana. If they were looking for him, as he said they were, he wouldn't be hard to spot. He was very tall for a Cuban, very thin, and had a unique triangular-shaped face. A few days before Christmas I told Claudio that if I didn't get back to the United States by the first of the year, the arms deal would probably fall through. Since we needed the money right away, I asked to be allowed to go to Escalona's headquarters to explain the situation to him. I was confident that the Comandante would come up with the necessary funds if I personally laid my plans before him. Claudio thought it was worth a try, and said I could go to Escalona's camp with the next courier run, which was to leave the day after Christmas.

A big fiesta was being planned for Christmas Eve. We would have a feast with roast pork, yuca, canned fruit, preserves, candy, rum, and wines made from papayas, bananas, and guavas. Another guerrilla band was to join us for the celebration. This outfit, six men who had taken to the hills around Soroa shortly after we left that area, arrived at our camp on December 23. The rains had finally stopped, and the sun shone brightly. The leader of the group, a man named Valdivia, was from San Cristóbal. One day he had driven a car to the entrance of that town's cuartel and asked the sentry for a light; as the soldier reached for a match, Valdivia pulled out a pistol and shot him. Valdivia was the first guerrilla I met who looked cruel. He was armed with a Star machine pistol; his men carried an assortment of shotguns and revolvers.

The party on Christmas Eve was great fun, but I was glad when Christmas had come and gone. On the morning of December 26 I left with Chicho and a peasant guide for Escalona's headquarters. We all shaved, wore civilian clothes, and carried revolvers. Claudio had given me a nice .38 Police Special for the trip, and Chico, on my advice, had exchanged his automatic for a .357 Magnum. There was no need to carry food since we would eat with peasants along the way. On the first day we walked in the morning, rested in the afternoon, and walked most of the night. After dark especially we made good time on the wide dirt roads that skirted the sierra.

On the afternoon of the second day we arrived at Captain Pepito's camp in the cattle country near La Mulata. Pepito had operated in that open terrain as early as election day. In a grove of trees lay several ballot boxes with their tops ajar, their former contents strewn on the ground about them; the captain and his men had sequestered the boxes from the local precincts on the night of November 3. Now, in the last week of December, Pepito was back in the vicinity looking for a place to land an aircraft carrying arms. The pasture land was open enough, but it was rolling and seemed not to have any long stretches of level ground. Pepito, however, had picked out a possible runway, which he wanted me to look at.

Although it wasn't too rough, the strip was very short: less than two hundred yards. Nevertheless, there was a pretty good approach and, drawing on my eight hours' experience at the controls of a Piper J-3, I surmised that a single-engined plane might be able to land there. But, I told Pepito, the pilot would really have to have cojones. In order to bring the aircraft to a complete stop he would probably have to crash it into the wooded slope at the end of the field. Moreover, even if he managed to land the plane undamaged, he would probably never be able to get up enough speed on that strip to take off. Pepito asked me to write down my observations so he could send them to the people who were arranging the shipment. He added that it might be necessary to seize and hold a stretch of highway for the airlift, and I agreed.

We left Pepito's camp before dawn on December 28 and re-entered the sierra as day was breaking. Slowly we made our way up a mountain that rose precipitously from the valley of San Diego de los Baños. Near the summit we encountered one of Escalona's sentries. It was almost noon, but the sky was overcast and it was quite chilly; the poor guard, a small peasant in his forties, was shivering. After chatting with him for a few minutes, we struck out on a trail that wound around the mountain, dipped into a little valley, and then went up a narrow canyon through which a small stream flowed. It took nearly two hours to cover the distance between the first guard post and Escalona's main camp. Along the way we passed four *emboscadas*, each manned by four or five guerrillas, with a submachine gun in every group. This was Escalona's way of insuring that he would never again be surprised by the enemy.

The Comandante embraced me warmly. So did César, who was now his adjutant with the rank of captain. They had been in that location since October, and the camp had an air of permanence. Some seventy men were well dispersed in squad-sized units; latrines had been dug and there were pits for incinerating garbage. Wood was collected and stacked as fuel for cooking and for warming fires. Escalona's portable kerosene stoves, unlike Claudio's, were used only when it was impossible to start a wood fire. The Comandante, César, Franco, and Cienfueguero slept in a cave in hammocks that hung from wooden posts. The entrance to the cave was like that of a tunnel: it was level and sufficiently large to enable a man to walk in without stooping, and it let in light during the day. There was a kerosene lantern for nighttime, and a large *26 de Julio* flag was displayed on a limestone wall. Escalona gave me a hammock and invited me to hang it in the command cave.

That night he and I discussed the arms situation. Claudio had not told him that I had left the island.

"You have been to the United States," Escalona said, somewhat surprised.

"I went and I returned."

"*Chico*, you can be very useful to us. *Muy útil.* We need arms and you can help us get them. Five thousand pesos is nothing. We will buy more *armas* than that."

"I am ready to go north at any moment."

"*Bueno.* I shall have to make some arrangements. The Revolution is entering a very critical phase. They are fighting hard in Las Villas. Already *el Che* has captured Sancti Spíritus."

This was the first I had heard of the rebel offensive in Las Villas. Sancti Spíritus, the third largest city in the province, was occupied on Christmas Eve. Escalona and his staff had been following the action on their Zenith Transoceanic, listening to rebel short-wave broadcasts from Las Villas and Oriente. Comandante Ernesto "Che" Guevara had moved out of the Sierra del Escambray the week before Christmas, and by December 28 he had overrun several cuarteles and had seized enough weapons to arm hundreds of peasants and town militiamen. He was now organizing an army at Placetas, preparing to march on Santa Clara, the provincial capital thirty-five kilometers away. In the northeastern corner of the province Comandante Camilo Cienfuegos, who was supposed to be on his way to Pinar del Río, was besieging the garrison at Yaguajay. Already the cuarteles at Remedios and the port of Caibarién had fallen to the rebels in northern Las Villas.

In Oriente every remaining batistiano strongpoint was under siege. Fidel was at Palma Soriano directing operations against the local cuartel. Since the first of the month, fourteen towns including Puerto Padre on the Atlantic coast, had been liberated with great quantities of arms taken. With Escalona and the others I listened as the female voice of Radio Rebelde read off a long list of weapons captured in some of the recent actions.

"What a shame," I said, "that they cannot send us some of those arms."

"We shall have arms," Escalona said. "You will bring them to us."

The next day, December 29, the Comandante dispatched

a messenger to Pinar del Río City. In a few days, he assured me, all the arrangements would be made for me to go *al norte*.

By the end of December my earlier unfavorable opinion of Escalona had changed. I still couldn't understand why he had ordered Claudio to cease operations, but I realized the necessity for conserving our forces and building a secure base of operations in the province, which Escalona obviously had accomplished. His headquarters area was virtually impregnable to either ground or air attack. Claudio was secure in the sierra to the east; Pepito, in the lowlands to the north, could always fall back on the headquarters area if pressed. Escalona's highly mobile smaller units were dispersed along the southern rim of the mountains: there was a fairly well-armed band under Captain Antonio in the Pica Pica region, and Captain Valdivia had returned to the Soroa area after Christmas, his group augmented by a number of Claudio's neophytes.

What impressed me most about Escalona during those last days of December was the loyalty, respect, and genuine affection which his officers felt toward him. Captain César, the adjutant, Captain Franco, the headquarters area commander, and Lieutenant Tellería, the officer in charge of security, were intelligent and educated men. César had gone to the University in Havana; the other two had attended the high school in Pinar del Río City. They were not the type to be awed by the posturings of an empty-headed martinet from Oriente. There was much more to the Comandante than I had perceived. Behind the bombast

—which was normal in Cuban politics, and Escalona's mission was as much political as military—was an honest and sensitive man who returned loyalty with loyalty, friendship with friendship.

I was beginning to realize that the Cuban Revolution was held together more by personal ties than by ideology. Fidel was free to discard principles, for there was no abstraction that would cause commanders like Escalona to betray Fidel or captains like César to betray Escalona. Material considerations were unlikely to lead to mutiny in the fidelista army because the great majority of officers were not propertied men; no matter what course the Revolution might take when it achieved power, they stood to gain. "What we need," Tellería told me, "is twenty years of revolutionary government."

The dawn of this new era seemed to be rapidly approaching as 1958 drew to a close. Radio Rebelde continued to report an almost unbroken string of fidelista victories. The Revolution was big news in the United States, as I learned when I picked up American stations on the AM band of Escalona's Transoceanic. The Cuban situation provided the lead story for Edward R. Murrow's New Year's Eve broadcast. The rebels, Murrow said, appeared to be halted in their offensive. He cited reports from Santa Clara that heavy government reinforcements had joined the battle that was raging around that city. Rebel radio broadcasts, Murrow continued, seemed to indicate that Castro's forces were pulling back in several sectors. On the short-wave band we heard some frantic combat transmissions from Las Villas that tended to confirm what Murrow said.

"Calling Cuban Red Cross, Cuban Red Cross. . . ."

"Listen here, chico, we have six comrades badly wounded out at kilometer sixteen. . . ."

"O.K.! O.K.! We shall try to send a truck out for them. In the name of God, tell your people not to shoot at us. . . ."

"Calling Comandante William Morgan! Comandante William Morgan! . . . "

"Hear me! Hear me! Send us reinforcements. We need help—ammunition! If we stay here they will wipe us out. We are going to move north. . . ."

It was impossible to follow the action from these broadcasts. I tuned in Radio Continental from Caracas, Venezuela, and the news was good: the fidelista offensive was continuing. The rosiest picture was painted by Radio Moscow: "Cuban revolutionary forces have now occupied most of Santa Clara. Heavy reinforcements sent from Havana by Dictator Batista were ambushed and completely wiped out this afternoon by Cuban patriots. A revolutionary column is now in Matanzas province marching on Havana. Other popular forces have entered the city of Santiago in Oriente province. . . ."

A newscaster in Dallas had a different story: "Seenyor Castro is finding out that the Cuban people don't love him after all. The uprising against President Batista that Castro has been calling for is not coming off. Government tanks and planes have smashed the rebel offensive and sent Castro's bearded warriors fleeing back to their mountain hideouts. . . ."

The eleven o'clock CBS news stated without qualification that "forces loyal to President Batista of Cuba have defeated a large rebel force at Santa Clara." CBS had been informed that government forces that night were making plans to

push on the next morning in vigorous pursuit of the fleeing rebels. Spokesmen for Batista, CBS said, "expressed
confidence that the two-year-old Cuban civil war is near-
ing its end." When I retired to my hammock shortly
before midnight on December 31, I did not foresee a very
happy new year.

7 NEW YEAR'S DAY MORNING, AFTER gulping down a cup of coffee, I turned on the radio to catch the seven o'clock news from Key West. There was a little static but the message was clear: Batista had fled the island of Cuba.

"Escalona!" I shouted. "*¡Batista salió!*"

For a moment the Comandante seemed to be paralyzed, his face frozen in an astonished stare. Then he gave a little leap into the air and began yelling to the guerrillas down the hill. *¡El Hombre se fué!* "The Man has gone!"

I turned the volume as high as it would go and began translating: "Before going into exile in the Dominican Republic, President Batista left the government of Cuba in the hands of a military junta headed by General Cantillo. This, however, probably does not mean an end to the Cuban civil war, as the junta is composed of members of Batista's political party. They can be expected to continue most of the policies of the Batista government. . . ."

We switched to the frequencies of the rebels in Las Villas, where we heard men joking and congratulating themselves. We tried to pick up Radio Rebelde in Oriente, but that station apparently wasn't on the air. Cuban commercial radio was playing popular music, except for Radio Reloj, which followed its usual format of alternating news briefs and short commercials accompanied by a ticking clock. The only item of interest was that something important was expected from a news conference called for nine o'clock that morning at Camp Columbia, the big military installation in the suburbs of Havana.

Escalona decided it was time for him to move out of the mountains. He did not abandon all caution, however; Franco and about thirty men were detailed to hold the base camp. The rest of us set out to join Pepito in the lowlands near La Mulata. I marched at the head of the column with the rifle-toting Comandante and César, who carried a Sten gun and, on a strap over his shoulder, a transistor radio tuned to Havana's most powerful commercial station, CMQ. Around ten o'clock the radio announced that Batista had resigned and that a junta headed by General Cantillo had named Dr. Carlos Piedra, then senior justice of the Supreme Court, President of the Republic. Apparently all was calm in Havana.

Cantillo, I thought, must have thousands of troops patrolling the streets of the capital; otherwise the underground would by now have seized the radio stations. Later I learned that the General had declared a unilateral cease fire and had confined his soldiers to Camp Columbia; even the police were barricaded inside their cuarteles. The underground militia did not venture into the streets until nearly two hours after the first looters had appeared and demonstrated that there was nothing to fear from Batista's army or the police.

About noon, when we stopped for lunch at a peasant's house at the foot of the sierra, we heard that the radio stations in Havana were finally taken over by the underground. Excited voices ordered militiamen of the Revolutionary Directorate and of the 26 of July Movement to report to their units. All other citizens were to remain indoors; any businesses open on that holiday were to close immediately. When not talking, the rebels played the stirring Cuban national anthem, *La Bayamesa*.

Escalona had no choice but to attack the government forces in an attempt to seize the province of Pinar del Río for the 26 de Julio. He planned to reduce the smaller garrisons on the northern highway one by one, thereby gaining enough weapons to arm the peasants and acquire the strength necessary to beseige the regimental headquarters camp near Pinar del Río. The peasant militia had gotten the word; as we sat eating lunch, machete-carrying peasants were drawn to us like flies, both from the hills and from the plains. Down the side of one mountain came a group of three or four on foot and one on horseback; the mounted man held aloft a 26 of July flag that was as big as his horse. All were welcomed and told to fall in with the guerrillas, who in many cases were their brothers or sons. It was a picturesque column that marched on Las Pozas that bright and sunny afternoon of January 1, 1959.

Shortly past three o'clock Fidel Castro's voice came over the radio. We halted our march to listen. Fidel had instructions for "all comandantes of the Rebel Army and for the people." Regardless of the news from Havana, the Maximum Leader said, "our troops must not cease fire at any moment. Our forces must pursue their operations against the enemy on all battlefronts. We will concede parleys only to those garrisons that wish to surrender."

Fidel said that apparently there had been a coup d'état in Havana, but added that the people should ignore it and take orders only from his headquarters. "The dictatorship has been overthrown as a consequence of the crushing defeats suffered in recent weeks, but this does not mean that the Revolution is now triumphant." Rebel Army operations, Fidel emphasized, would continue until he called them off—and that would be "when the military elements that have risen up in the capital put themselves under the orders of the revolutionary headquarters. Revolution, *sí!* Coup d'état, no!"

Fidel went on to warn against attempts to snatch the victory away from the people. "The democratic victory," he said, "has to be absolute." The workers of Cuba must prepare themselves for a general strike. "The people and the Rebel Army must be more united and firmer than ever so as not to let slip away the victory that has cost so much blood."

Escalona remarked that Fidel was very perceptive. The *militares* in Havana might accept Manuel Urrutia, Fidel's choice for President—with Cantillo as chief of the armed forces. But we were not fighting for *Urrutia con Cantillo.* We wanted Urrutia alone—*Urrutia con aire*—and thus had to continue forward.

Pepito joined us before sunset. We had more than two hundred men when we reached Las Pozas in the last glow of twilight. In the dark the enemy couldn't see how poorly we were armed. After deploying some guerrillas along the highway in front of the cuartel, Escalona demanded that the enemy commander come out for a parley within fifteen minutes or we would open fire. He set up his command post in a peasant's hut beside a dirt road a few hundred yards south of the cuartel. When the enemy commander,

Lieutenant Otero, came out to talk, he was escorted to this hut, where Escalona had staked out some of his best-armed men.

Otero was a handsome, curly-headed young man. He wore a fatigue uniform without a hat and in an open holster on his hip carried a .45 automatic. He and the bearded Escalona sat down at a rough table in the dirt-floored bohío to negotiate in the yellow light of a kerosene lantern. Pepito and Cienfueguero, armed with submachine guns, stood inside, while César and I looked on from the doorway, and others peered through the windows.

I was impressed by Otero; he looked and acted like a soldier. He addressed Escalona respectfully as Comandante. He said he was as anxious as anyone to prevent further bloodshed. But as a military man he had to do his duty. He couldn't surrender his garrison until his superiors ordered him to do so. He admitted he didn't know exactly who his superiors were at the moment; his regimental commander in Pinar de Río apparently had fled the country. Things were very confused in Havana. These matters should be clarified during the night. He asked Escalona to hold off his attack at least until morning.

Our people had marched far, Escalona said; although alert, we were tired. Otero's garrison was surrounded; he and his men could go nowhere and no reinforcements could reach them. The lieutenant would gain nothing from the delay, while we could get some needed rest. Very well, Escalona agreed, we would not open fire until dawn.

When Otero had returned to his cuartel, Escalona conferred with Pepito in the bohío while César and I sat down with the radio on a grassy bank beside the road to catch up on the news. The Santa Clara garrison had surrendered to Che Guevara around noon. In a desperate effort to save his crumbling army from the fidelistas, General Cantillo had sent a plane to the Isle of Pines to fetch ex-Colonel Ramón Barquín from the national penitentiary. Barquín, who had been convicted of plotting against Batista in 1956, was liberated on the afternoon of January 1, 1959, and flown to Camp Columbia where General Cantillo restored his rank and turned over to him command of the Cuban Army. Barquín made a statement to the press which César and I heard on the radio a little before nine o'clock. "Doctors Fidel Castro and Manuel Urrutia may come to Camp Columbia when they desire," the new army chief said, "in order that the latter may take charge of the presidency of the Republic."

It sounded to me as if our victory had been complete. "If Urrutia is going to be the President of the Republic," I said to César, "as an American citizen I cannot serve him."

"Of course you can; you are one of us."

"No. What I mean is that I would lose my American citizenship if I served the government of another country. *Un ciudadano americano* may be a revolutionary in another country, but not a soldier in the armed forces of that country."

"But it does not matter," César said. "We shall give you Cuban citizenship. I am sure that Escalona will not let you go, because we need you now more than ever. We will acquire from the batistianos great quantities of modern war matériel which you must teach our peasants how to use. In reality the Revolution is just beginning. And it is not certain that the fight against the army of Batista is yet over. Barquín said he would give the presidency to Urrutia, but he did not say he would give the command of the army to Fidel."

"But Barquín is a good person, a revolutionary, is he not?"

"He appears to be. But he is still a *militar*. He must surrender the army to us so we can purge it of all the bad elements. Otherwise Urrutia could be overthrown by a *golpe de estado*, as Prío was in '52."

"*Bueno*, the Revolution must triumph completely, that is certain. But I want you, as adjutant of the column, to take note that on this day I have given you my resignation. If you do not accept it—well, I have no desire to be hanged as a deserter."

César smiled and said he would convey my resignation to Escalona.

In the first light of January 2, Otero's jeep, a large white flag fluttering from the aerial, came barreling down the road toward Escalona's command post. He came to announce that he was ready to surrender his garrison. By that time we had commandeered some trucks and a car, and these vehicles, loaded with guerrillas and peasants, followed Otero back to the cuartel. The face of the yellow concrete building still bore the marks of the bullets that had been splattered against it three months before. César and I strode through the portal behind Escalona and Otero. About two dozen troops were drawn up in the courtyard. They were unarmed and stood at parade rest as Escalona harangued them.

This was the dawn of a new day for Cuba, the Comandante declared to the forlorn soldiers. He listed some of the many things the Revolution would do for the nation. A tremendous task was at hand. The Revolution needed the help of all worthy sons of the fatherland, including those soldiers whose records were clean. Go home to your families, he told the former batistianos, and await the call. The troops were dismissed and replaced by half a dozen peasants and three guerrillas, one of whom Escalona promoted to lieutenant and designated garrison commander. The other two veterans were to serve as *clases*, or noncommissioned officers.

In the sierra there had been no corporals or sergeants because Batista had held these ranks before he promoted himself to colonel and, later, general. In January 1959, when the Rebel Army became the Army of the Republic its commanders recognized the need for noncoms. Officer grades, however, continued to be restricted to those never held by the ex-dictator: lieutenant, captain, and comandante—a rank equivalent in status to that of major in the American army but with command functions not normally assigned to an American major. At Las Pozas Comandante Escalona began taking over a regiment, an outfit usually commanded by a colonel.

Escalona was grateful to Otero for making the first step so easy. The army lieutenant offered to accompany the guerrilla commander to the other cuarteles on the northern highway to try to persuade them also to surrender peacefully. Escalona accepted the offer, and gave Otero a 26 of July armband. In the meantime Cienfueguero was distributing weapons from the Las Pozas cuartel's arms room. Escalona noticed that I still had only a .38 stuck in my belt. *¡Óyeme!* he called to Cienfueguero. "Give the American an *arma*. Give him a good one. Give him a Garand."

Escalona considered the Garand—the American M-1 semi-automatic rifle—to be the best weapon ever invented. Perhaps it was, but after shouldering one of those nine-and-a-half-pound rifles for three years at The Citadel and half a year at Fort Benning, I would have preferred something lighter and more dashing, like a Madsen submachine gun. Nevertheless, as a good soldier I accepted what was given me. It was an M-1 rifle, all right, but the word "Roma" was stamped on the receiver. Batista had bought it from the Italians.

The arms from Las Pozas doubled our firepower, and we lost no time in setting out for the next cuartel. We formed a caravan of three stake-bodied trucks led by a Chevrolet sedan. I rode in the car, driven by a guerrilla named Manolo who had no front teeth, with Escalona, Otero, César, and Cienfueguero. The latter was also missing some teeth; he was a happy, broad-faced peasant who nevertheless was deadly serious about his job as the Comandante's bodyguard.

La Mulata contained only a small police station. No one there was in any mood to resist. After Escalona detailed a few men to take charge of the town, we pushed on to Consolación del Norte. This town, which the natives called La Palma, had the largest army garrison between Bahía Honda and Pinar del Río City. Franco was from La Palma. Poor Franco, I thought, he was sitting up there in the sierra guarding Escalona's camp while we were liberating his home town. La Palma had a population of about three thousand, most of whom seemed to be in the streets when the Rebel Army rolled in at about nine o'clock. The mood was festive: many of the people were wearing 26 of July armbands. When we appeared, they cheered and shouted *vivas.* The cuartel was on a little hill. A mulatto soldier was sitting in a chair on the porch, his rifle across his lap, talking to a mulatto woman. The sentry rose when Escalona and Otero approached, but didn't challenge them. An officer met them at the main entrance and within a few minutes the surrender was arranged. Escalona repeated his Las Pozas speech, dismissed the batistiano troops, and replaced them with a dozen men from his column. We appropriated about fifty individual weapons and several heavy machine guns from the La Palma cuartel.

We pushed on to the village of San Vicente and then to Viñales, where we found the cuartel already in the hands of the rebel underground militia. Escalona conferred with the militia leader, who, though he called himself comandante, accepted a lieutenant from our column as commander of the garrison. Escalona detached a dozen *barbudos*—bearded ones—to back up his lieutenant. All along our route, through towns, villages, the countryside, people lined the road clapping, cheering, and waving Cuban and 26 of July flags.

It was about noon when we reached the outskirts of Pinar del Río City, where we were met by representatives of the local underground. They informed us that the police station was already in the hands of the local militia and that the batistiano army commander wanted to talk with Escalona about surrendering his six-hundred-man garrison. The underground had arranged to feed and house our troops at the local high school in case we couldn't immediately occupy the army barracks. Escalona decided to have his men fortify the high school and eat lunch there, while he made a personal reconnaissance in the area of the cuartel. Tellería was detailed to take the column to the school, and Otero was sent with him to show the men how to set up the heavy machine guns. The leader of the underground joined us in Escalona's car for a drive by the army base, which was on the central highway just east of its intersection with the northern highway.

The regimental encampment was formidable. About a dozen fortress-like buildings were strung out along a ridge surrounded by several hundred acres of open ground, all of which was enclosed by a high chain-link fence topped with barbed wire. We drove past the main gate on the highway where a number of civilians were talking with the sentries. "Before we enter," Escalona announced, "we shall eat some lunch."

We drove up to a highway restaurant which was closed in obedience to Fidel's general strike order. The owner, who lived on the premises, was persuaded to serve the revolutionary chief of the province and his staff. We each had a shot of cognac before lunch and beer with the meal: pan-fried steaks, rice, and a salad of cold string beans and onions. Thus fortified, we proceeded to the cuartel to demand its surrender.

As the car came to a halt at the main gate, Escalona stuck his head out of the window and introduced himself to the sentry and stated his business. Before the perplexed soldier could reply, the sergeant of the guard appeared. He saluted the rebel comandante and asked us to please wait one little moment while he telephoned Lieutenant-Colonel Cué, the acting base commander. Civilians clustered around the car to get a close look at the barbudos. Most seemed afraid to speak, but one little boy asked for a bullet as a souvenir. "Later, chico," Cienfueguero replied. "We may need all we have."

In less than a minute the sergeant of the guard was back. He signaled to the sentry to open the gate for our car. Colonel Cué, the sergeant informed Escalona, was in the second large building on the right, the *jefatura*. As we approached the building it became clear that we weren't the only outsiders who had been admitted to the compound that day. It was like open house at the jefatura. There were delegations of business leaders, labor leaders, churchmen, women—all of whom came to make demands or offer unsolicited advice to Colonel Cué. There were even some representatives of the Directorio Revolucionario: a bearded youth who wore a large Cuban flag as a cape and strutted around with an automatic pistol in his hand, followed at a respectful couple of paces by two less flamboyantly attired boys of about fourteen. That kid's mother, I thought, must have hidden him for at least two months while he grew that beard.

Lieutenant-Colonel Cué, a trim, middle-aged man in a fatigue uniform, was desperately trying to keep his command intact and maintain his bargaining position with whatever government might emerge in Havana. On the afternoon of January 2 it was becoming increasingly clear that the new government would be 100 per cent fidelista. Nevertheless, Cué still clung to the hope that in Havana Colonel Barquín could work out some compromise that would save the army from the fidelistas. Barquín, however, was ready to throw in the towel; the fidelistas had already seized every important military post in the three eastern provinces except the army and navy bases at Cienfuegos— which were in the hands of the *Segundo Frente del Escambray*. As Escalona was advancing in Pinar del Río, three fidelista columns from Las Villas were seizing cuarteles in Matanzas. Barquín knew that nothing, not even an alliance of the army in Havana with every non-fidelista revolutionary group in the capital, could resist the onslaught from the provinces. Early in the afternoon, just before we arrived at Cué's jefatura, Barquín declared that he would turn over the Cuban army to Fidel's newly appointed chief of staff: Comandante Camilo Cienfuegos. Camilo, the radio announced, was expected in Camp Columbia before sundown.

Militarily, Cué's position in the province of Pinar del Río was similar to Barquín's in Cuba: he still controlled the largest garrison, but his outlying units were rapidly being picked off by the fidelistas who dominated the countryside. While Escalona was moving on Pinar del Río City, Valdivia descended on San Cristóbal and Candelaria. Antonio was in Los Palacios. Claudio sent Juan Díaz to take Bahía Honda, while he himself led the rest of his band to Cabañas, Artemisa, and Guanajay. On January 2 the cuarteles in all these towns were occupied by barbudos of the 26 of July Movement. But Cué still held on in the provincial capital.

The colonel acknowledged to Escalona that he had heard that Camilo was to be the new army chief of staff, but added that he had no official confirmation. He could not turn over his command to Escalona until he received orders from Camp Columbia to do so. Escalona assured the colonel that as soon as Camilo was installed as *jefe del estado mayor*, he would issue the orders. In that case, Cué asked, would it not be better to wait for the orders? Escalona didn't want to wait, but there was nothing else he could do: to launch an attack under these circumstances would be criminal.

"Tomorrow morning," Escalona told the colonel, "I am coming here with my men to occupy this cuartel—regardless of what you hear from Havana. In the meantime I am going to station some of my men at the guard post."

"I have no objection," the colonel said smoothly.

Cué walked with Escalona outside the jefatura, where members of the various delegations were milling about.

"I want you to throw these people out of here," Escalona said.

"With much pleasure."

Escalona and Cué agreed that nobody would be allowed through the gates unless he had a pass personally signed by either one of them. The meeting ended cordially. We got into our car and drove directly to the high school.

The school was a large, two-story, flat-roofed structure built around a paved courtyard. The classrooms, which could accommodate perhaps four hundred students, were now used as dormitories for half that many fidelistas. Desks were moved out to the verandas or to the courtyard to make room for guerrilla bedrolls. A few town boys joined us at the school, though most of the local revolutionaries congregated at the police station a few blocks away. I spotted a .50 caliber machine gun in the courtyard, and asked Escalona if he'd like me to set it up. "Yes," he said, "take it up to the roof." Escalona detailed three men to serve on my machine gun crew. As soon as we were on the roof, I traded one of them my M-1 rifle for his carbine.

That night Escalona gave me permission to use the high school's telephone to call the United States. I talked with my wife, explaining that I would be tied up with the

Revolution for a while longer. Perhaps I could return to the States before the semester was over at the University of Michigan. If I were detained beyond that, we agreed that she should join me in Cuba at the end of the month.

The next morning, January 3, Escalona gave me a special mission. Instead of going along with him to occupy the regimental cuartel, I was to load my machine gun crew and a squad of riflemen on a truck and take them to the town of Los Palacios, where Captain Antonio was having problems with Major Jacinto Menocal, one of Batista's most notorious murderers. Escalona said that Menocal, who was holed up in the local cuartel with a few of his men, refused to surrender to the revolutionary forces. "I want you to go to Los Palacios and bring back Menocal— dead or alive. And when you go, you go as a lieutenant."

It was roughly an hour's drive to Los Palacios. I rode in the back of the truck with the troops. We acknowledged the applause of the peasants who gathered along the highway. The main street of Los Palacios was filled with people. I swung down from the truck as it stopped, and walked up to a fat man in a green uniform. I introduced myself to the perspiring militiaman as Lieutenant Americano of *la tropa de Escalona;* I had come to help capture Menocal. The man snapped to a spread-legged version of attention and saluted.

"*Bueno, teniente,*" the man said, "Menocal is already dead. They have the body over there."

"And the cuartel," I asked, returning his salute, "is it occupied?"

"*Sí, señor.* It was occupied yesterday."

The information Escalona had passed on to me, like most revolutionary communications in those confused days, was

not entirely correct. Menocal, whose base was San Cristóbal, had passed through Los Palacios in an automobile with
one or more of his men on the morning of January 1. They
were on their way to Dayaniguas, on the Caribbean coast,
where an American-owned rice plantation kept a crop-
duster aircraft which they hoped to commandeer for a flight
to the United States. The manager of the plantation, a
man named Joe Alley, informed the fugitives that the
plane's pilot was away for the holiday and might not be
back until the following morning. Menocal was willing to
wait but his accomplices weren't; they abandoned their
leader and fled north in the automobile. Joe Alley also
slipped away in his car, leaving the infamous major stranded
at the plantation.

By this time the underground militia had risen up in
Los Palacios and Captain Antonio was descending from the
hills of Pica Pica. On the night of January 1, when the
militiamen learned that Menocal was in Dayaniguas, they
broke their nonviolent siege of the cuartel and rushed
south to hunt the "Jackal of San Cristóbal." They cornered
him on the plantation, in Joe Alley's frame house. Throughout the next day Menocal traded shots with the militiamen
who surrounded the house. At dusk Captain Antonio arrived from Los Palacios, where he had accepted the surrender of the cuartel.

Early on the night of January 2, Menocal apparently
slipped out of the wooden house and into an adjacent
rubble-stone structure, the plantation's business office. At
dawn Antonio along with a few of his men advanced
against the stone outhouse aboard a bulldozer, the blade
of which was raised high to shield them from the major's
bullets. The tractor was driven by Antonio's second-in-

command, whose *nom de guerre* was Pedro Buldoza. When they battered down the walls of the office, they discovered Menocal wasn't there. Apparently, he had sneaked back into the house, where he had committed suicide hours before the bulldozer assault on the office. Antonio's men found him in the house with a bullet hole in his temple that must have been made by the pistol in his hand. The rebels added a few more holes to the lifeless body, then threw it into a station wagon which Antonio drove to Los Palacios. When I arrived at Los Palacios, people had gathered in the street to gawk at the corpse in the back of Antonio's vehicle. Shots were fired into the air in celebration as militiamen and barbudos posed for news photographers from Havana.

I pushed my way through the crowd and congratulated Antonio, who was sitting behind the wheel of the station wagon. After contemplating the blood-caked body for a few moments, I announced that Escalona had told me to bring it back to Pinar del Río.

"I shall take it to Pinar," Antonio said firmly.

"But Escalona said for me to bring it back."

"*Yo lo llevo,*" Antonio repeated. He gunned the motor, the crowd parted, and away he went. We returned to Pinar del Río City without Menocal.

While I was in Los Palacios, Escalona had occupied the regimental cuartel outside the provincial capital. Lieutenant-Colonel Cué had skipped out during the night, and there were only a few overage lieutenants around to greet their conquerors. Our Comandante entered the camp with eighty men, having left the others at the high school. The enemy officers, clerks, cooks, barbers, and bartenders were allowed to remain on the base to serve the Revolution, but all the combat troops were dismissed.

That afternoon I visited the post exchange, which was now run by a bearded lieutenant named Abilio who had joined the officer corps that morning. I told Abilio about my own promotion, mentioning that I guessed I'd better go see Escalona and find out whether I was a first or second lieutenant.

"Do not preoccupy yourself," he said. "It must be first. Here, take a pair of these." He handed me the insignia of first lieutenant, the rank which I assumed without bothering to consult the Comandante and which I held until March 23, 1959.

8 BY JANUARY 3 ALL ARMY POSTS
from Pinar del Río City to the Havana border were commanded by veteran guerrillas who took orders from Escalona. Most of the police stations, however, were in the hands of the underground, and Escalona made no move to deprive the militiamen of these spoils. But in the provincial capital, when he moved to the army base on the outskirts of the city, he took the precaution of leaving a strong contingent of barbudos at the high school. The main objective of the Rebel Army in Pinar del Río, as in all of Cuba, was now to neutralize whatever strategic advantages other resistance elements might have achieved since the flight of Batista, and to insure that no further gains were made by rival revolutionary groups.

On January 4, Escalona learned that armed followers of Carlos Prío had landed at the ex-President's farm on the coast near Bahía Honda. Franco and his men, who had descended from the sierra two days before, were sent to disarm the *priístas*. The leader of the group, which had sailed from Florida on January 2, told Franco that they had come to help assure the success of the Revolution. Franco in turn informed the recent arrivals that the success of the Revolution was already assured and proceeded to relieve them of their weapons.

While Franco was at Prío's farm, I was sent to occupy the town of La Coloma on the Caribbean coast. Escalona had heard that the local militia was allowing some batistiano bigshots to embark there for Mexico or the United States. I was to impound all the boats, arrest any suspicious characters, and leave a squad of fidelistas to garrison the town. With about thirty men I entered La Coloma shortly before noon. The local citizenry welcomed us as liberators, ushering us to a banquet table they had set up in the town plaza. We ate a magnificent lunch, impounded a few rickety boats, and arrested no one. Six barbudos were left in charge of the town while the rest of us returned to Pinar del Río City that afternoon.

When I reported in at the jefatura, César informed me that an American had been arrested at the municipal airport. He and I drove to the airport to interrogate the prisoner—a smiling Minnesotan of about thirty, fair and somewhat paunchy—who had landed that afternoon at the controls of a twin-engined Beechcraft loaded with rifles and machine guns. The pilot, a man named Leslie Bradley, explained that he had been contacted by the 26 of July Movement to fly the arms to Pinar del Río before the fall of Batista. Bradley told us he had kept the rebel-owned weapons in his Miami apartment for several weeks while he waited for the Movement to tell him where in the province to land them. He was afraid the Feds were closing in on him in Miami, so he decided on his own to deliver the arms to the revolutionary authorities at the Pinar del Río airport.

We took Bradley to the jefatura where we found his underground contact, Danny Hernández, who corroborated his story. César apologized for the inconvenience and returned a Smith & Wesson automatic that had been taken from Bradley at the airport. The pistol was a new model of advanced design; it was like a marvelous toy to its owner, who proudly demonstrated its novel features to the revolutionaries at the jefatura. Not long afterward, he left with his friend Danny to spend a few days at the Hernández family plantation near San Juan y Martínez in the Vuelta Abajo, Pinar del Río's fabulous tobacco district.

The next morning Escalona had a mission for me: to return to the high school to arrest Lieutenant Otero, who was to be put in the regimental stockade. This was at a time when people were being apprehended all over the province. Both military and civilian jails were rapidly being filled. The motive behind these mass arrests seemed to be to stop the flight from the country of those who may have been involved in "war crimes." Otero didn't appear to be the criminal type; eventually, I thought, it would be established that he was innocent of any bastistiano atrocities. Meanwhile, I had to take him into custody. I chose Juan de Dios, a country boy who had served in the sierra with Escalona, to help me make the arrest and deliver the prisoner.

Juan de Dios said he knew how to drive a jeep. It turned out, however, that he wasn't used to driving on city streets. He gave me a few scares as he narrowly avoided collisions with pedestrians and passing motorists. Parking our jeep in front of the high school, the two of us walked up the stairs to the roof where Otero and two militiamen were manning a heavy .30 caliber machine gun. Neither Juan de Dios nor I drew our revolvers. "Otero," I announced, "Escalona has told me to bring you prisoner back to the cuartel."

"Very well," he said calmly, as if he had been expecting us and had long ago resolved to submit peacefully. He rose to his feet, unbuckled his pistol belt, and gave it to Juan de Dios.

"I will have to take the *brazalete* also," I said. He removed his 26 of July armband and handed it to me.

Otero followed Juan de Dios to the jeep and I walked behind him. The prisoner rode in the front with the driver while I occupied the rear seat. We delivered Otero to Bigote, the regimental jailer, who put him in a large cell with about a dozen other former batistiano officers and soldiers. Through the bars I asked the ex-lieutenant if there was anything I could do for him—could I get him some cigars, or magazines? No, he replied, and thanked me.

"Well, if you need anything, ask Bigote to get in contact with me and I shall be happy to get it for you, if I can." I wished him luck. At the jefatura I found Escalona had left, but César was there, and he told me why I had been ordered to arrest Otero.

According to César, four students from the Catholic University in Havana had fallen into the hands of Captain Iturriaga in Bahía Honda on the day after Christmas. Although unarmed, the students were carrying messages from Havana to the underground in Pinar del Río City. Iturriaga had them tortured in Bahía Honda. When he was satisfied that he had gotten from them all the information possible, he sent them to the cuartel at Las Pozas with instructions to Otero to dispose of them. The lieutenant ordered his men to take the four boys into the woods and hang them and bury them. When the soldiers refused to obey the order, Otero declared they would receive no supper that night, December 27, nor any other meals until the deed was done. The order was finally carried out just before dawn. The bodies were buried on a lower slope of Pan de Guajaibón—where they were found a week later by revolutionary investigators.

"Then it looks like we are going to shoot Otero," I said to César.

"Probably. But he will be given a trial first. We shall start the trials in this province next week. What we need to do now is to start training a firing squad. Naturally, you are the one best qualified to do this. . . ." He paused, as if he had asked a question and awaited an answer.

"*Bueno.* I am willing to teach the *fusileros* how to shoot, but I do not want to give the command to fire. It would be very bad for a foreigner to do that. It must be done by one of you who have suffered so much from these *asesinos.*"

"I agree," César said quickly. "One of us will take charge of the executions. We only want you to train the riflemen. You know their aim is very bad."

"Okay. Who are the people you want me to train?"

"Well, you could look around and pick out the men you think best. You could form your own platoon."

"*Gracias,* but no. The truth is, César, that I do not wish to command a platoon of *verdugos.*"

"But it would not be that. It would be a commando

platoon. You would have armored cars and all the heavy weapons. There is a tank down in the motor pool; you would have that also. Yours would be the armored platoon, ready to move quickly to wherever it is required. Naturally we would expect your men to be so well trained in rifle marksmanship that we could call upon them to form a firing squad when the need arises."

"In that case it seems good to me. I should like to have Juan de Dios as platoon sergeant."

César said he would give orders to Rogelio, the officer in charge of the armory, to turn over to me or to Juan de Dios all the weapons we needed. At the motor pool we could select the vehicles we wanted. We first went to the armory where we found about a dozen tripod-mounted machine guns, an 81 millimeter mortar, and a pair of 37 millimeter pack howitzers. I told Rogelio that we would be back for these weapons as soon as we had organized the platoon; at that time we would also pick up about two dozen Garand rifles and some grenades. There were several crates of rifle grenades and hand grenades in the armory; from an open box I selected a pair of hand grenades to tie on to my pistol belt.

At the motor pool there were two jeeps—one with a mounted .50 caliber machine gun—two armored scout cars, and a light tank. All the vehicles ran well, according to the mechanic, except the tank, which had a broken transmission. I told him to get busy and fix the tank, since we were taking over all the vehicles and needed them in top condition. Crawling inside the tank, I found a helmet on the driver's seat. It was just what I was looking for, the finishing touch, a piece of distinctive headgear. Other rebel officers wore berets, cowboy hats, or fatigue caps; I would wear a tanker's helmet. Now that we knew what equipment we had, we began choosing our men. We needed about thirty, of whom at least eight could drive. I left the selection of the men to Juan de Dios, though I suggested that some of those who accompanied us to Los Palacios or La Coloma might be good prospects. He started recruiting that night. The next morning, as I was leaving the mess hall after breakfast, I ran into Escalona, who asked what I was doing. I told him that I was preparing to organize the commando platoon. "Very good," he said. "But perhaps it can wait. I am going to Havana today. Would you like to go with me?" "Yes, indeed. There will be no problem. Juan de Dios can organize the people without me." I greatly looked forward to joining the Comandante, his bodyguard, and his chauffeur on the excursion to Havana.

We arrived in Havana early on the afternoon of January 6. Our first stop was at Camp Columbia where Escalona hoped to talk with Comandante Camilo Cienfuegos. Camp Columbia was a larger edition of our regimental base in Pinar del Río; it had the same neat and sturdy military architecture and plenty of open spaces. Barbudos and militiamen wearing a highly individual assortment of green uniforms and armed with a variety of weapons lounged about. A few unarmed civilians and men dressed in the khaki of Batista's army wandered around.

We learned that Camilo had left the base for an inspection tour of the city and Havana province. He was not expected back until night, so Escalona decided to drive across town to see Che Guevara at La Cabaña fortress. Che had taken over La Cabaña, the Cuban army's artillery headquarters, on January 2, the same day that Camilo assumed command at Camp Columbia.

Fidel had yet to arrive in Havana. The Maximum Leader was slowly making his way along the Central Highway from Oriente, stopping at all the towns and cities on the way. He was preparing for a showdown with the rival revolutionaries in Havana by rallying the people of the provinces behind him, making sure that the military posts along his route were in the hands of 26 of July barbudos. The guerrillas of the Directorio Revolucionario, three or four hundred in all, had abandoned Las Villas and were now camped out at the University of Havana. The Segundo Frente del Escambray still held the coastal city of Cienfuegos—which Fidel bypassed—but a contingent of Frente veterans had appeared in Havana and occupied the Vedado high school.

The underground militiamen who had chased about the city during the first three days of the month were no longer roaming the streets. Camilo had put some under military discipline, posting them at Camp Columbia or at various police stations; others had been disarmed and sent home. Some had joined the non-fidelista guerrillas at the University or at the high school. There were undoubtedly many others—including followers of ex-President Prío—who had simply taken their guns and gone home to await further developments.

The general strike had ended on Sunday, January 4. When we arrived in Havana two days later, the city appeared normal, except that the policemen now wore 26 of July uniforms. The only concentrations of armed men who still refused to put themselves under Camilo's orders were at the high school and the University. Escalona decided to stop off at the University on our way to La Cabaña to reconnoiter the Revolutionary Directorate's encampment.

The rebels at the University were quite different from the peasant and working-class barbudos and militiamen of Pinar del Río and Camp Columbia. The fidelistas, when they were not performing assigned tasks, looked like vagrants; the troops at the University, even when they were idle, seemed to be going about some enormously important business. They were intense, animated young men with ideas and strong convictions. Many were standing around in small groups debating among themselves. As we walked by, they would lower their voices or stop talking. Obviously they regarded us with suspicion, if not hostility. Cienfueguero and Manolo, the driver, both of whom were missing front teeth, clearly didn't belong at the University. Escalona with his neatly trimmed beard and I with my ridiculous tanker's helmet might have passed as Directorio rebels had we not worn 26 de Julio insignia. Our rivals sported shoulder patches with *13 de Marzo*, or simply *13*, written in white across a blue and red background. The date commemorated the Directorate's attack on the Presidential Palace in 1957. The University rebels carried rifles or submachine guns. They had several vehicles that resembled light tanks but had rubber tires; these had been captured from the batistianos in Las Villas. No one challenged us or even spoke to us; after wandering around a bit we returned to the car, and drove off to La Cabaña.

La Cabaña is an eighteenth-century fort built on a bluff on the east side of the Havana channel. Until Batista constructed a tunnel under the channel, La Cabaña was not directly accessible from Havana, though the Presidential Palace and most of the other government buildings in the city were well within the range of the fort's guns, mostly field artillery pieces. Behind the ancient breastworks was a modern military camp. There, in the headquarters building, we found Comandante Che Guevara.

El Che was receiving visitors. A line about a block long and composed mostly of upper-class Cuban ladies and their teen-age daughters led into Che's jefatura. We politely pushed our way through these elegant, ecstatic females and into the building. Che was alone in a little office, sitting behind a big desk that was pushed up against the doorway to keep the visiting women at a distance. The famous *guerrillero* stood up and motioned to us to come in. Escalona climbed over the desk to embrace his old comrade from the Sierra Maestra. Then he introduced Manolo, Cienfueguero, and me. I was presented to Che as *un americano que es un revolucionario de carajo*. Che smiled pleasantly, nodding to each of us. He was reserved but not cold. He wore a loose-fitting fatigue uniform and had a black sling around his neck; he said that his arm had been hurt in Las Villas but that it was better now and he really didn't need the sling. With all the feminine clamor in the hall, conversation was difficult. After a few minutes we moved the desk aside and closed the door in the disappointed faces of Che's admirers. The shutters of the one window in the room were closed.

"We have just left the University," Escalona said. "They have some little tanks there. Do you think they're going to create any problems?"

"*Bueno, chico,*" Che replied, "I do not know. They are probably angry about last night when Camilo made them give up the Presidential Palace."

Members of the Directorio Revolucionario had seized the Presidential Palace on January 1. They declared that they would turn it over to Urrutia—but only after Fidel's President-designate agreed to rule in conjunction with a legislative body composed of representatives of all the revolutionary groups and civic organizations. Fidel would not allow Urrutia to negotiate with the D.R. After landing in Havana on the afternoon of January 5, Urrutia went directly to Camilo's headquarters at Camp Columbia. Camilo then declared martial law in Havana, announcing it would remain in effect until Urrutia was installed in the Presidential Palace. Three members of the President's cabinet—which was composed of men who served at Fidel's pleasure, and not as representatives of organizations—were allowed to go to the Palace to talk with the boys of the Directorate. The emissaries returned to Camp Columbia with the news that the D.R. was ready to surrender the Palace to Urrutia unconditionally. The President took possession of the Palace that night, a squad of Camilo's men moved in to guard him, and the martial law was lifted.

The D.R. was now confined to the campus of the University. "It would be best to let them remain there until Fidel arrives," Che said.

"*Bueno,*" Escalona drawled, "Fidel will not have to preoccupy himself with Pinar del Río. It is under our control 100 per cent."

All of us were puffing on cigars in Che's office, which by now was thick with smoke. To relieve the situation, Che opened the shutters. Immediately three shrieking teenaged girls tried to climb through the window. As Che closed the shutters, Escalona announced that it was time for us to go. We said goodbye, opened the door carefully, replaced the desk, and left the hero of Santa Clara to contend with his fans.

Of the thirty men Sergeant Juan de Dios selected for our platoon, some were guerrilla veterans, but more were fidelista militiamen from the area of Pinar del Río City. They were mostly boys from poor families who wanted to stay in the army. They realized that most of the militiamen would be sent home as soon as Fidel consolidated his control over the island; since they regarded my platoon as a permanent organization, they were eager to join it.

I spent several days instructing the men on the mechanics of rifles and machine guns as well as drilling them in infantry tactics. Those who showed the greatest aptitude were appointed squad leaders. One of these, I later learned, had been a batistiano soldier until January 1, when he put on a 26 of July armband and fell in with the militia. He, like other ex-soldiers who tried the same trick, was discharged as soon as he was found out. The urban militia was at best loosely organized, and probably a majority of the fidelista militiamen joined the Movement on January 1 or 2.

Fidel's forces continued to be officially called the "Rebel Army"—not the "Revolutionary Army." The word "revolutionary" had been so weakened through constant misuse by Cuban *políticos* that Fidel and his soldiers remained "rebels" even after they were masters of the island. Some members of the old army—the Army of Cuba—served in the Rebel Army in Pinar del Río after January 3, though none of them in combat units. But by May 1959 Escalona had discharged all former batistiano officers and soldiers from his regiment.

The men from the old army who were still around in January, knowing that they faced an uncertain future, tried very hard to please us. The cooks produced some delicious soups—especially *ajiaco* and *fabada*. The barbers took great care in their work. As he cut my hair one poor fellow told me that he had planned to retire that year after twenty years' service; not only was his pension now in doubt, but his automobile, which he had saved for many years to buy, was among the cars impounded on the parade ground. Of course I could do nothing about his pension, but I told the barber that I would speak with César about his car. César, however, was not moved.

"These people," he patiently explained to me, "have lived a good life serving those who oppressed the Cuban people. It is true that they personally did not murder or torture, but they accepted money from those who did. In this sense all their property is ill-gotten. It will be disposed of as the Revolution sees fit."

On the base all property, private as well as public, was taken over by the rebels. The families of batistiano officers and noncoms were evicted from their government housing,

which was then occupied by Escalona's officers and their
families. Escalona himself lived in the base commander's
mansion with his mother and sister, who arrived from Oriente in mid-January. I slept in the barracks with the troops
until the end of the month, at which time my wife came
to Cuba and we moved in with Escalona.

We received no pay until the end of January, but no
money was needed on the base. There were free movies in
the regimental theater almost every night, and at the Officers' Club I could sign for drinks and cigars. The Officers'
Club was open to all members of the Rebel Army, although
many enlisted men—and some officers—didn't use their
bar privileges because they couldn't bear the embarrass-
ment of telling the bartender that they couldn't sign their
names. Almost everyone, however, enjoyed playing domi-
noes or watching television at the Officers' Club. On the
night of January 8 the place was packed when Fidel,
who had arrived in Havana that afternoon, made a tele-
vised speech from Camp Columbia.

The gates of Camp Columbia had been thrown open to
the public, and roughly forty thousand *habaneros* gathered
there to hear the Maximum Leader. Someone released three
white doves, symbols of peace, one of which landed on
Fidel's shoulder where it remained for much of his two-
hour speech. Fidel called for unity, self-sacrifice, discipline,
peace, and disarmament. "The greatest crime that could be
committed today in Cuba," he declared, "would be a crime
against the peace. . . . Whosoever would not be ready to
renounce something for peace—whosoever would not be
ready to renounce everything for peace in this hour—is a
criminal and a traitor." A certain group which called itself

revolutionary, Fidel said, had stolen a large quantity of arms from the army training camp at San Antonio de los Baños in Havana province. The Maximum Leader demanded the immediate return of these weapons and the disarmament of all "private armies." It wasn't until the next night that Fidel, when interviewed on the television program "Before the Press," launched a direct and devastating verbal attack on the Directorio Revolucianario.

I watched this show at the home of the Rev. Thomas Willey, Sr., Free Will Baptist missionary. On the morning of January 9 a soldier brought me the message that there were some americanos at the main gate who wanted to see me. The visitors were the Rev. Willey; his son Tommy, also a minister; his daughter-in-law Ruth; and his granddaughter, Alicia. A tall and powerful man of about sixty who looked more like a Texas cattle baron than a preacher, Rev. Willey said he and his family had heard me on the radio (I recalled a local newsman had taped a few of my words at the high school). They had been praying for a rebel victory, and now they wanted especially to thank me, one of their countrymen, for what I had done for the cause. I gave the Willeys a tour of the base in my jeep. Tommy had a camera and along with some of my men, I posed with his two-year-old daughter on our tank. The Willeys invited me to dinner that night at their mission about ten miles north of the city; I readily accepted.

At dinner Mrs. Willey, Sr., a handsome woman some years younger than her husband, noted that I had built up a great deal of good will for myself and advised me to consider settling in the area. "These people are completely sincere," she said.

Tommy and his father agreed that there were many opportunities around Pinar del Río for an enterprising American with the right connections. They mentioned three Yankees who had made more than a million dollars over the last three years raising tomatoes which they shipped to the United States during the winter. Since every two or three years a frost wipes out a good portion of the Florida tomato crop, a man can make a killing growing tomatoes in Cuba, where it never freezes. Cattle and rice were also good businesses. The Willeys had among their friends many prosperous farmers and ranchers who could help me to get started. The Revolution was confiscating a lot of good land that belonged to Batista's henchmen. I should be able to buy or lease some of this land from the government. These were interesting thoughts, and I discussed them at length with the Willeys and their friends over the next few weeks. That night, however, the discussion was broken off when Fidel appeared on "Before the Press."

During the broadcast, Fidel rejected the demands of the Directorio Revolucionario for the participation of the various resistance groups in the government of President Urrutia. He blamed the vexatious attitude of the Directorate on its leader, Faure Chomón. The D.R. chief claimed to be a comandante, but Fidel never used that title nor the word *compañero*—comrade—in referring to him. He was always Señor Chomón. He accused Chomón of engineering the robbery of some five hundred rifles and machine guns and eighty thousand rounds of ammunition from the cuartel at San Antonio de los Baños. What did Chomón plan to do with those arms? Fidel advised him to surrender all his arms, evacuate the campus of the University, and disband his little army immediately. The same went for the Segundo Frente del Escambray, led by Señor Eloy Gutiérrez Menoyo. Mixing sarcasm with righteous indignation, Fidel spoke with the confidence of a giant challenged by pygmies.

The next day Faure Chomón capitulated, ordering his men to lay down their arms. Gutiérrez Menoyo, who had made no demands on the government and had remained on the sidelines to watch the unfolding of events, quickly announced that his Segundo Frente would do the same; he claimed to have four thousand men under arms. Fidel allowed the D.R. to camp out in the University stadium for the weekend while the disarmament was carried out. The last of the Segundo Frente forces were demobilized a few days later in the city of Cienfuegos.

Faure Chomón accepted his humiliation and learned to follow the fidelista line; in 1960 he was named Cuban Ambassador to the Soviet Union. In the same year, however, Gutiérrez Menoyo and several of his comrades from the Segundo Frente began forming guerrilla bands to fight against the revolutionary government. It was a futile gesture; power in Cuba was as firmly in the hands of Fidel Castro and his fanatically loyal Rebel Army in 1960 as in 1959. The Revolution's first prime minister, José Miró Cardona, bowed to reality in February 1959, when he turned over his office to Fidel. Manuel Urrutia followed suit, resigning the presidency in July 1959. Other government officials meekly handed in their resignations when informed that they no longer had the confidence of the Maximum Leader. Miró, Urrutia, and their middle-class allies realized that they couldn't compete with Fidel in Cuba. They looked to the United States for salvation.

In January of 1959 it was by no means clear that Fidel intended to liquidate the Cuban bourgeoisie. But it was evident that he had the power to destroy anyone who might oppose him.

9 AFTER THE CAPITULATION OF THE Directorio Revolucionario and the Segundo Frente del Escambray, Fidel began to pare down his Rebel Army. In Pinar del Río, Escalona announced that most of our militiamen would be released on January 15. I suggested that it might be possible to discharge me then, too, since my men were organized and making progress on the firing range. They were already sufficiently trained so that any officer could supervise their practice. But Escalona didn't think so. He kept me in the Rebel Army for two more months.

A week after he had been arrested at the airport and released, Leslie Bradley came to see me. He presented me with a razor and the advice that I shave off my unattractive whiskers. I had to admit that my three weeks' growth of beard was pretty sparse and that I looked more like a First of January than a 26 of July rebel. After I shaved, we drove out to the Hernández family plantation in a car Leslie had borrowed from his hosts.

Danny Hernández lived with his parents in a luxurious home in the heart of the world's best tobacco land. There, where a man could make a fortune on just one acre, the Hernández family cultivated many, all carefully covered by cheesecloth tenting. "When I met Danny and his folks," Leslie said, "and they said they were working for the Revolution, I knew it wasn't a Communist revolution, and I didn't mind helping them."

Tobacco planting, which fascinated me, only mildly interested Leslie. If we decided to go into that business Danny's father would gladly help us get started; he even offered to lend us one of his foremen. But Leslie, more attracted to the sky than to the soil, talked about starting an air freight and passenger service between the Vuelta Abajo and Tampa, the American cigar-making capital. He also thought about applying for an air route between Pinar del Río and the Mexican state of Yucatán. As potential partners we discussed these and other projects on several occasions during the next few weeks.

When Leslie flew to the United States for a visit in late February, I gave him a box of *pinareño* cigars to take to my father-in-law. The cigars did not reach their destination. I never saw Leslie again, though in April, while I was in the United States, he did appear at the Willeys' mission looking for me. The missionaries told me he was driving a blue Cadillac and claimed to be the chief of the Nicaraguan Rebel Air Force. In 1960 he was arrested in Havana for "conspiring to invade Nicaragua." It seems that he had thrown in with the wrong Nicaraguan rebel faction—the anti-Communist one. The revolutionary government was not innocent of the crime for which it imprisoned Leslie. Before I was discharged from the Rebel Army in March 1959, Nicaraguan and Dominican exiles had received military training on our base in Pinar del Río. Many foreign adventurers were drawn to Cuba in those days.

Donald Soldini, whom I had not heard from in months, telephoned me from Havana around the middle of January

1959. The expedition he had gone to Mexico to join never materialized. He returned to Cuba as a tourist a few days after the fall of Batista. I didn't remind him of his vow to stay out of Cuba after the Revolution came to power. Soldini urged me to join him in Havana; he had the names of some informers we could go hunting for. I thanked him for the invitation but explained that I was tied up in Pinar del Río with army business. A few weeks later Soldini was arrested for wandering around the Presidential Palace with a rifle without authorization. His old friend Urrutia either couldn't or wouldn't save him from deportation. His banishment from Cuba wasn't permanent, however, for a year later I read in a Havana newspaper that he was on the Isle of Pines making a movie with Lon Chaney, Jr.

Revolutionary firing squads began mowing down batistianos in Oriente and Las Villas provinces in the first days of January 1959. The executions raised storms of protest in the United States as well as in some Latin American countries, but in Cuba no dissent was heard. The press seemed totally subservient to the new regime; it vigorously defended revolutionary justice against the attacks from abroad. *Bohemia*, Cuba's most popular magazine, ran gruesome photographs of scores of bodies that were recovered from hidden graves in the countryside, many in Pinar del Río. All were alleged to be victims of the batistianos, but I suspected that some might have been informers done in by the guerrillas.

As portrayed by the Havana press, the barbudos could

do no wrong. The habaneros were apparently enraptured by the quaint warriors who marched into their city early in January. "The great majority were humble peasants," *Bohemia* noted, "earnest and simple men, without ostentation of any kind, who blinked in amazement as they contemplated the towering and cold edifices of the capital and saw themselves applauded by the multitude at every step." The picturesque Comandante Camilo Cienfuegos, a native habanero, was a special favorite of the press. *Bohemia* published a captivating photograph of the Rebel Chief of Staff and his mother, whose simple print dress and lack of jewelry, makeup, and hair styling clearly marked her as a woman of the people—and very different from the sophisticated ladies whose pictures were the usual fare in that magazine.

The distance between country and city, between rich and poor, was less in Pinar del Río than in Havana, and consequently the rebels didn't offer quite the same enchantment. Nevertheless, rebel soldiers did cause excitement when they appeared on the streets of the provincial capital during January. Almost every weekday after January 12 my motorized platoon roared through the downtown area on its way to the rifle range east of the city. Warned of our approach by the broken muffler of the lead jeep, the citizens would gather on the sidewalks to cheer. Having discarded my tanker's helmet for an Afrika Korps-style forage cap, I sat in the jump seat of the first vehicle while a soldier swung on the .50 caliber machine gun behind me. We were followed by the two open armored cars, each with .50 calibers mounted fore and aft and carrying a squad of riflemen. Bringing up the rear was a jeep with a water-cooled .30 caliber machine gun. (I decided not to subject the downtown streets to the tread of the tank.) The applause decreased toward the end of the month, and by February only a few kids on the edge of town bothered to run to the road and shout their *vivas* at us. After Fidel Castro made his long-anticipated visit to the provincial capital, revolutionary fervor in Pinar del Río gradually declined.

Fidel and his entourage arrived at our base the night of January 17. The Maximum Leader had spent ten hours on the Central Highway between Havana and Pinar del Río City, speaking at every town and village along the hundred-mile route. When he walked into Escalona's house he was hoarse and bleary-eyed. His secretary was concerned because he was getting only about two hours of sleep a day, and was running a fever of 102 degrees. Nevertheless, he acted like someone who had never felt better in his life.

Escalona introduced me as "the American who is training the firing squad." Fidel thought that was a great joke. "The American who is training the firing squad?" He threw back his head and roared with laughter. As I stretched out my hand, he grabbed me by the shoulders and gave me a bear hug. Everybody was happy. Fidel kidded around with Escalona's sister and the other girls, mostly relatives of rebel officers who had been invited to the Comandante's home to meet the Maximum Leader. After awhile Fidel excused himself, and he and some members of his staff retired with Escalona to the breakfast room for a private dinner.

Fidel was a man of immense physical as well as mental

strength. His liberal adversaries, some of them great intellectuals, were no match for him because he knew Cuba as they could never know it; moreover, they didn't have his grasp of the physical dimension of politics. Son of a well-to-do but less than respectable family, Fidel spent most of his boyhood in rural Oriente. As a youth he was sent to Havana where he graduated from a Jesuit high school and then went on to earn a law degree at the University. Although an above-average student who excelled in sports, he was shunned by some classmates because of his uncouth habits. At the University he was known as *Bola de Churre,* or "Grease Ball." To me, however, he was very attractive.

After dinner at Escalona's, Fidel went to the City Hall plaza and delivered a two-hour speech to some thirty thousand people. With Escalona and about a dozen others, I stood on the platform with the speaker, who made his usual pitch for discipline and self-sacrifice. He also declared that, despite the protests from abroad, the executions of war criminals would continue. He charged that a campaign of vilification was being waged against the Cuban Revolution in some neighboring countries. But the truth about Cuba was being told by worthy foreign newsmen like Jules Dubois, of the *Chicago Tribune,* who happened to be standing on the platform and was introduced to the crowd.

Another American reporter who was present was Ruth Lloyd of WNEW Radio-TV in New York. After the speech Fidel agreed to grant WNEW a telephone interview. Ruth Lloyd placed the call to New York from the phone in Escalona's study. Fidel understood English fairly well, but he asked me to stand by as an interpreter. When questioned about the executions, he appealed to the American people for understanding. All the war criminals, he said, were getting fair trials. Fidel sounded like the stereotype of a Latin American revolutionist, and I doubted that he made a favorable impression on listeners in the United States. Even in Cuba he had to be seen to be appreciated; radio and the printed word conveyed little of his power. Television served him better, but it was primarily through personal contact that Fidel achieved his rapport with the masses.

The "war crimes" trials in Pinar del Río were to begin the week following Fidel's visit. Ruth Lloyd wanted me to phone in some three-minute reports on the trials; she said WNEW would give me $15 a report. I needed the money, but I wasn't sold on the idea. I didn't like the way her colleague in New York pressed me over the phone to say whether or not I would refuse to serve on a firing squad. WNEW's broadcasts from Cuba were written up by the wire services and sent all over the world. Anything I said on the radio was likely to get me in hot water either in the United States or in Cuba, so I decided not to make the reports.

The first "war criminals" sentenced to death in Pinar del Río were ex-Captain Iturriaga and eleven enlisted men who had served with him in Bahía Honda. On January 20 they were tried and convicted of the multiple murder of Cuban peasants. The trial was held in the regimental theater and was open to the public. The place was packed; I was standing at the rear of the theater, and the noise of the spectators made it difficult for me to follow the proceedings. I left before César, president of the tribunal, condemned the men to be shot. Eleven of the twelve death sentences were approved that night by the Minister of Justice in Havana. The batistianos faced a firing squad the next morning.

My men assembled outside the regimental jail at dawn on January 21. I selected the six best marksmen among them for the firing squad. The best, however, were none too good. They had done all right against a paper silhouette at twenty paces, but I was worried about the effect a live target would have on their aim. They were also accustomed to taking commands from me or from Juan de Dios, and I was afraid they might not respond well to Pepito, whom Escalona had assigned to give the firing orders. There was a definite possibility, I thought, that these first executions in Pinar del Río might be badly bungled. To guard against this I decided to join the firing squad. We took our places in a gully about two hundred yards from the jail. Pepito led Iturriaga and an ex-sergeant into the gully, placing both men about ten yards in front of my squad. Escalona, who was standing among several dozen spectators on the bank above, had decided to have the men shot two at a time. The arrangement lessened the chances of both being killed instantly, and my first inclination was to protest, but then I realized that this was Escalona's show and that I shouldn't interfere. If the batistianos lingered awhile in dying, that would be regrettable, but, after all, they themselves had never shown much compassion for their victims. I instructed two men to join me in shooting at Iturriaga and four to fire at the ex-sergeant.

Pepito, a personable fellow of about thirty who had

grown up on a sugar plantation in Oriente, did not relish his assignment. After blindfolding the two men, he asked Iturriaga if he'd like to command his own execution. A batistiano had made a big hit doing that before television cameras in Oriente, but Iturriaga was not interested in emulating him. He just stood there with a faint sneer on his face.

When Pepito gave the first command—*¡Atención!*—I knew we were in for trouble. His voice was loud enough, but the command was not sharp. The men were very raggedy in coming to attention.

¡Preparen! Again the order was slurred; eventually everyone came to port arms and threw his left foot forward.

¡Apunten! There was no snap, either in command or in the response.

¡Fuego! The rifles went off like a string of Chinese firecrackers. Iturriaga fell over backward and looked dead. The other man, however, only went down on one knee. Pepito forgot to give the command to order arms and my M-1 rifle remained at my shoulder; impulsively, I took a bead on the wounded batistiano. But then Pepito walked over to the kneeling man and killed him with a pistol shot through the right temple. I lowered my rifle and ordered the men to lock the safeties and come to parade rest. Pepito concluded his performance by administering a perfunctory *coup de grâce* to Iturriaga and muttering *La guerra es de carajo.* Escalona applauded by drawing his Browning automatic pistol and firing fourteen shots in the air.

Escalona agreed that the nine remaining condemned men should be shot singly, with Juan de Dios giving the firing orders. These executions went smoothly. Three days later there was another batch of "war criminals" to be disposed of. For these and those who followed them in death, the place of execution was to be the base pistol range, which had both a *paredón*—a concrete wall capable of stopping rifle slugs—and bleachers for the spectators.

My men's performance under the command of Juan de Dios convinced me that my presence at the executions was no longer necessary after the first day. Thereafter I would deliver the squad to the pistol range on the appointed mornings, turn the outfit over to Juan de Dios, and go directly to breakfast. On my way to the mess hall I often would pass one or two hearses bearing coffins for the men whose executions were forthcoming. Usually I would be drinking my *café con leche* as the sound of the first volley reverberated across the camp. The only condemned man whom I cared anything about was Otero. On the morning of his execution I waited at the pistol range until the jailers brought him down.

"Adiós, Otero," I said as I put my arm around his shoulder. His hands were tied in front of him.

"Adiós, lieutenant." He paused barely a second before voluntarily resuming his march to the *paredón*. He didn't want anyone to think he was stalling; like most of those who died there, he was a brave man.

Tommy Willey and his father did some proselytizing among the prisoners on the base and won quite a few converts. I tried to notify my friends in advance of every execution so that they could be on hand to minister to the condemned in their final hour. One of them, the late Major Menocal's chauffeur, died with a New Testament in his hands. The Willeys also worked the provincial prison on the north side of town, where most of the fifty-odd men accused of capital crimes were kept before being brought to the military camp for trial and probable execution. My friend Monolo, with whom I had stayed in Havana, was the chief investigator and commander of the police guard at the provincial prison, while the civilian administrator there was the Rev. Luis Díaz, minister of the Church of God and a former underground leader.

The doomed batistianos weren't the only ones who died violently. Before the executions began a militiaman managed to commit suicide by hanging himself from a double-decker bunk in the barracks; in order to accomplish this extraordinary feat he must have dived off the bunk head first. Later Bigote, the regimental jailer, for some unknown reason blew his brains out. A guard at the provincial prison was killed by the accidental discharge of a submachine gun. There were too many guns around, I thought; when they weren't killing us, they were reminding us of death. I stopped wearing my pistol and ordered my men not to carry side arms off duty. Juan de Dios protested. "We must have our revolvers when we go to town," he said. "In town they say that it is the people of the American who *fusilan*. There are relatives of the batistianos everywhere. We must protect ourselves."

After commanding more than two dozen executions, Juan de Dios was getting jumpy. I rescinded my no-side-arms order. Escalona, who had dropped in on the last performance of the firing squad, informed me that the men were a bit shaky. My presence, he thought, might steady them. Reluctantly I agreed to attend the next executions. On the appointed morning I took a front-row seat in the bleachers next to Captain Antonio. There were two men scheduled to die that day.

The first was a tall, handsome mulatto. As he stood blindfolded before the paredón, his hands bound in front of him, he said in a loud but serene voice, "*Muchachos*, the only crime you are going to commit is to kill me, because I am innocent." Six rifles fired but not a single shot touched him. He stood as calmly after the volley as before. The spectators gasped, the men of the firing squad trembled. Juan de Dios seemed paralyzed. I borrowed Antonio's .38 automatic and, as I stepped onto the field, shouted, "Ready! Aim! Fire!"

This time the man went down. I went up to him immediately, commanding the squad to order arms as I walked. There were bullet holes in his shirt and he seemed dead, but I wasted no time in putting the automatic to his head and pulled the trigger. It made a neat round hole.

Next to die was a Negro who was hauled kicking and screaming to the paredón. The jailers were unable to blindfold him, so I told them to throw him up against the wall and get out of the way. There was no post to which the prisoner might be tied; several target stands were near the wall but they were only two or three inches thick, much too frail for this purpose. The condemned man froze in terror when, his jailers having abandoned him, he saw his executioners arrayed before him.

"Ready!"

The command jolted him out of his trance. "No! No!" he cried. "Do not get ready!" He tried to climb the wall.

"Aim!"

"Do not aim! No!" He tried to hide behind one of the target stands. The gun muzzles tracked him relentlessly.

"Fire!" The riflemen were steady; they had no qualms about this one. He turned his head and ducked just as the guns went off. Most of the bullets struck him in profile, tearing away his nose, lips, chin, and most of his cheeks. His face was transformed into a raw, red mass of flesh and bone that contrasted sharply to the smooth black skin bordering it. He lay on his back with what was left of his face turned to the firing squad. Anyone that hideously blasted, I thought, had to be dead.

"Well," I commented as I walked forward, "it is not necessary to give him the *tiro de gracia*."

"Yes, americano!" one of my men shouted. "Give him the shot! He still lives!" His arms and legs were twitching. His movement ceased only when a bullet from my pistol entered his skull.

All the men on the firing squad that day were routinely excused from the next round of executions. I fixed it so that most of them would never have to serve again. Juan de Dios still occasionally performed the unpleasant task of commanding the squad, but another sergeant, Armando, was increasingly assigned this responsibility. Armando, a former militiaman, was older and more mature than the barbudo Juan de Dios.

Early in February, Carlos, whom Claudio had sent to Havana to raise money in December, appeared at regimental headquarters wearing a lieutenant's uniform. Earlier in January he had rejoined Claudio in Guanajay, where he had been stationed ever since. He didn't like it there, and wanted to transfer to our base; Claudio, he said, had agreed to let him go if we had a place for him. Carlos explained that he had been unable to complete his fund-raising mission in December because, the Havana underground being at the time in disarray, it was very difficult to find the proper people.

After I told César that I could use Carlos as executive officer of my commando outfit, he agreed to put through the transfer. I planned to groom Carlos as my successor and then resubmit my resignation to Escalona. But Carlos didn't work out; he got along poorly with both the peasants and working-class soldiers of the platoon. The men began to complain to me about his arbitrariness and arrogance. It wasn't long after he joined us that he mentioned he was thinking of applying for a transfer to Havana. I agreed to support his application. After Carlos departed, I started training Armando to take over the platoon.

Armando demonstrated his ability to run the outfit when I came down with the mumps. Escalona cautioned that the disease was very serious for a man of my age, and insisted that I remain in bed until all the swelling was gone. For nearly a week I was confined to a second-floor bedroom in the Comandante's house, where I was nursed by my wife. It was during this period that Alberto Bayo, the Spanish Republican officer who had trained Fidel and Che in Mexico, paid a visit to the base. César brought him to see me. I sat on the edge of the bed as we discussed the Spaniard's plans to reorganize the Rebel Army into mobile hundred-man companies. Bayo was short and a bit rotund, but very military in bearing, with a neatly trimmed grey beard and wearing the blue uniform of a brigadier general of the Spanish Republican Air Force.

On March 22 I reminded Escalona of my desire to leave the Rebel Army. The commando platoon, I assured him, functioned beautifully without me. I would be very grateful if he would discharge me immediately because the United States Embassy in Havana had announced that Americans who remained in the Rebel Army might lose their citizenship. I loved Cuba, yet I could not forsake my own country; I was no *vendepatria*. There was also the matter of my wife: our baby was due soon and she wanted her father, who was a doctor, to deliver it. Cuban médicos, of course, were very good, but she naturally had more confidence in her father. Besides, we both desired that the child be born on U.S. soil. If we waited much longer, my wife would be unable to travel.

Escalona said he would come to a decision that night. When I appeared at headquarters a little after eight o'clock the next morning, I learned that he and César had already left the base on business. But Escalona had instructed Franco, the chief of the post, to process my discharge. The necessary forms were completed. Franco reminded me that my third paycheck—$125, the monthly salary of all rebel officers—would arrive in about a week.

"By that time," I said, "I shall be in the United States. Of course, I shall return after the baby is born, but do not keep the check for me. Donate it to the Agrarian Reform."

A month and a day later, according to a newspaper story that my wife's aunt read to me in New Hampshire, the "United States warned . . . that any of its citizens who serve in the Cuban armed forces face possible loss of citizenship. The embassy [in Havana] issued a warning in a public statement, quoting instructions of the State Department and the Immigration Act." This was the second notice, and I was glad that I had gotten out of the Rebel Army after the first one. I didn't think the State Department would try to punish anyone who had heeded its first warning. That would be an act of bad faith that, for some reason, I didn't believe our government was capable of.

10 FIDEL PROMULGATED THE AGRARIAN
Reform Law on May 17, 1959, nine days before I returned
to Cuba. The decree established the National Institute of
Agrarian Reform (INRA), outlawed large landholdings—
one thousand to three thousand acres, depending on land
use—and promised each peasant family a "vital minimum"
of sixty-six acres. I knew that a man could do very well
planting sixty-six acres in tomatoes; if the land was suitable
for tobacco, he could even make a fortune. As a landless
peasant from *Carolina del Sur* and a veteran of the Rebel
Army, I asked the revolutionary government for sixty-six
acres. I took my request to Escalona and César, who not
only welcomed it but assured me that it would be granted.

César had been named chief of INRA zone PR-2, with
headquarters in San Cristóbal. He suggested that I look for
a farm in his zone, where much land had already been
confiscated from the batistianos. For a couple of weeks I
lived with César and his mother on a confiscated ranch
near San Cristóbal. One day Escalona dropped by on his
way from Havana to Pinar del Río City to announce that
"Fidel says to give the americano what he wants." I selected a plot of about sixty-five acres that fronted on the
central highway and was part of Los Pinos, an immense
plantation that had been jointly owned by some friends

and relatives of Batista. INRA was now forming a co-operative to plant tomatoes on Los Pinos. Even though I elected not to join the cooperative, INRA gave me virtually unlimited credit.

There was no house on my land so I chose as a residence the former country home of Pepe Fraga, Batista's chief of parking meters in Havana. It was a nicely furnished brick and stucco home set among thirty acres of citrus and avocado trees; the finca was on the central highway near Candelaria, ten miles from my land at Los Pinos. César said I could live there rent-free until I got around to building my own home. A peasant family lived in a frame house on the place and took care of the fruit trees; we got along very well. Late in July my wife and infant son joined me there. Part of my wife's savings was used to purchase a new Fiat 600 automobile; the rest bought food and other necessities until we began to market our tomato crop in December.

We sold more than $20,000 worth of tomatoes and cucumbers, mostly through brokers at the Farmers' Market in Pompano Beach, Florida. Inexperience, however, led to inefficiency, and our net profit on the 1959–1960 crop was only $3,300. We hoped to do much better the next year; I had plans to buy up produce from local farmers to ship to the United States under our label. But by the end of the 1959–1960 crop year, it became obvious that private export agriculture—and practically all individual enterprise—was doomed in Cuba.

Since I had expected some collectivization of Cuban agriculture, the formation of the first "cooperatives," which resembled the *ejidos* of post-revolutionary Mexico, didn't disturb me. In fact, I was delighted by the great social benefits—increased employment, schools, medical clinics, "people's stores"—that they brought to the long-neglected Cuban peasants. As long as there were still some commercial farms operated by individuals or private corporations, these, I felt, would prove more productive than the state-managed "cooperatives"—without reverting to the pre-revolutionary exploitation of the peasantry—and eventually lead the government to de-emphasize collectivization. That, at any rate, was what had happened in Mexico. During his first year in power, Fidel seemed willing to allow capitalism to coexist with state enterprise. Toward the end of 1959, however, there were indications that the socialist current in the revolutionary government was running very strong.

In October, César, who was now INRA chief of the entire province, stopped by San Cristóbal to drink a cup of coffee with me. He was returning from a meeting in Havana with Fidel and all the INRA provincial chiefs. He had received a new gospel which, in his gentle way, he proceeded to preach to me.

"As Fidel said, we must create in the people a new mentality—a collectivist mentality."

"Well," I answered, "I am in accord that we must promote the unity of the people—that all must work for the common good of the country. But some do this better by working on their own account. I am one of these. I am an individualist."

"I am, too," César said, smiling pleasantly and patting me on the shoulder. We broke off the discussion because, I think, neither of us wanted to admit to the other—or to himself—that the systems to which we were respectively committed were incompatible. Within a month of our conversation came the resignation and imprisonment of

Comandante Hubert Matos, military chief of Camagüey, who charged that the INRA organization in his province was heavily infiltrated with Communists; the mysterious disappearance of Comandante Camilo Cienfuegos on a flight from Camagüey to Havana; the dismissal of most pro-capitalist ministers from the revolutionary government; and the appointment of Che Guevara as president of the Cuban National Bank. I gave scant thought to these events at the time; I was more concerned with supervising the labors of some forty peasants who were working in my tomato fields.

I saw Fidel twice during the winter of 1959–1960. On each occasion he was very friendly and inquired about the progress of my crop. The first time, at a ranch near San Cristóbal, he held our son and said he was a beautiful baby. The second time, at Los Pinos, he introduced me to Anastas Mikoyan, First Deputy Premier of the Soviet Union. Mikoyan, who was making a "good will" visit to Cuba, smiled wanly when Fidel explained to him what I was doing.

In the spring of 1960 Cuban newspapers were suppressed, a former Rebel Army captain was executed for counter-revolutionary activity, and Fidel accused the United States government of plotting against his regime. Peasants were trucked into Havana to wave their machetes in defiance of Yankee imperialism and intimidate what was left of the Cuban bourgeoisie. The socialization of the economy continued apace. In June, as National Bank president, Che Guevara proclaimed a state export monopoly: henceforth all Cuban exports were to be marketed abroad by the government, which would retain all hard currency gained through these sales and compensate private producers with rapidly depreciating Cuban pesos. These developments convinced my wife and me that the kind of life we wanted was no longer possible in Cuba. We decided to abandon our farm, for which we had never received a title, and return to the United States in July.

It was on July 13 that the U.S. Department of State admitted defeat in its underhanded attempt to deprive me of my citizenship. In the fall of 1959 our embassy in Havana announced that all American citizens residing in Cuba should register with the nearest United States consul. The consulate at the embassy was the closest to our residence, so I went there on October 14 to register my wife, my son, and myself. Since a census was to be taken in the United States in 1960, I thought that the registration of Americans abroad was related to the national head count. I anticipated that the consul might refuse to enroll me, claiming that I had lost my citizenship by serving with the Cuban armed forces, so I brought along my Rebel Army discharge paper, which proved that my service had ended a month before the embassy issued its second warning, and a more recent document from the army's Investigative Department that identified me as a private American citizen engaged in farming near San Cristóbal.

At the embassy a thin, disheveled woman of about forty gave me a registration form, and I went to a nearby table to fill it out. One item asked if I was then, or had ever been, a member of the armed forces of a nation other than the United States; if the answer was "yes," I was required to attach a statement. The woman who had given me the form said she would take my statement; she asked me questions and typed as I replied. I told her when I joined the Rebel Army, whom I served under, and when I was discharged. She didn't ask me when it was that I first tried to resign, or if my service was voluntary after January 1; from Lieutenant Wallace's international law class at The Citadel I knew that one did not forfeit his American citizenship by serving against his will in the armed forces of a foreign nation. I answered a lot of questions about my rank, pay, uniform, and present activities, and declared that I had never taken an oath of allegiance to the Cuban government. The typed statement she produced from the answers was pretty messy; there were numerous strikeovers and insertions, which I offered to initial, but she said that wouldn't be necessary. The document, however, had to be notarized.

I was sworn in by the U.S. Consul, a severe, mannish female named Eleanor A. Burnett, and signed the statement in her presence. Neither Miss Burnett nor the woman who typed the affidavit warned me that it might be used in an attempt to legally expatriate me. I suspected that they had this in mind, but doubted that the embassy or the State Department would choose to take such drastic action against someone who had so conscientiously complied with their orders. Besides, I knew that an affidavit that appeared to be altered couldn't be admitted as evidence in an American Army court-martial; certainly it wouldn't stand up in a civilian court. I willingly surrendered my passport to Miss Burnett and allowed her to copy my Rebel Army documents on her Thermofax machine. Although I didn't need the passport to travel between Cuba and the United States, I asked Miss Burnett to mail it to me as soon as they were through with it.

It was nearly five months later that my wife received a form letter signed by Miss Burnett stating that "it is a pleasure to inform you that your application for registration as an American citizen which was executed at this office has been approved by the Department of State in Washington." I didn't hear from the embassy until several days later. "In connection with your pending citizenship case," Miss Burnett wrote on March 7, 1960, "would you kindly furnish the address in the United States at which you last resided." Until I received this letter, I didn't know that I had a "pending citizenship case."

In my reply to the Consul I gave my parents' address as my last American residence; I also offered to supply any other information, "in writing or personal testimony," that she might require. "As an American citizen subject to the laws of the United States, I am, as I have always been, fully disposed to cooperate with the legally constituted authorities of the United States and to obey all valid orders and injunctions of these authorities. Should the State Department elect to take some action against my citizenship, I would greatly appreciate notification as soon as possible, along with an official copy of my affidavit and a receipt for my passport."

Miss Burnett acknowledged receipt of my passport, adding that I could have a copy of the affidavit for $2.50. She didn't need any more information. "The available evidence," she wrote on March 22, "shows that you served voluntarily in the Cuban Armed Forces on and after January 2, 1959." The Department of State, she regretted to inform me, "has disapproved your application for registration. The Embassy has been instructed to prepare a certificate of loss of nationality . . . under the provisions of Section 349 (a) (3) of the Immigration and Nationality Act for submission to the Department for consideration." I knew that any evidence that I had served voluntarily after January 1 was false; but they weren't going to let me see the "evidence" nor even allow me to testify in my defense. The certificate of loss of nationality had been prepared on March 4—three days before Miss Burnett wrote to me mentioning that I had a "pending case." All they needed now was the signature of some functionary in Washington to condemn me to citizenless status.

I was saved from this fate by Travis Medlock, a young South Carolina lawyer with a passion for personal freedom. We first met at ROTC camp in 1954, and had carried on an intermittent correspondence since that time. Although we disagreed on many political and social issues, we both recognized and deplored the steadily mounting threat to individual freedom by mindless and soulless bureaucracies. My case offered Travis an opportunity to strike at the cumbersome and insensitive machinery of the State Department. Stung by its failure to prevent the radicalization of Cuba, the Department was venting its rage upon a lone American citizen. Travis refused to accept a fee and insisted on paying his own expenses.

The first thing Travis needed to prepare our case was a copy of my affidavit, for which I sent a $2.50 Cuban money order to Miss Burnett. My letter with the money order was received on March 30, but it wasn't until April 12, after the embassy got a forceful letter from Travis, that the document was finally mailed to me. Obviously the people in the embassy were stalling; they were trying to keep their "evidence" out of our hands until their colleagues in Washington had de-Americanized me. Miss Burnett, who had bungled the job of taking my statement in October, was removed from the case in March, after inadvertently revealing that star-chamber proceedings were underway against me. Our new adversary was one Wayne R. Gilchrist, the new American consul. The document Gilchrist sent me was not a photocopy of the affidavit; it was a laboriously executed and certified typescript which failed to show any of the strikeovers or insertions of the original.

The bureaucrats' attitude convinced Travis that we had little chance of stopping them from executing the certificate of loss of nationality. As soon as this had been done, however, he would petition a federal judge for a writ of habeas corpus to release me from illegal detention abroad, and would contend that the Immigration and Nationality Act didn't provide the "due process" guaranteed by the Constitution. Both of us were enthusiastic about the case, which, we thought, might become a landmark of constitutional law. Travis, however, felt that our challenge to the constitutionality of the Immigration and Nationality Act would be stronger if we could show that I had exhausted all possible administrative remedies before going to court. He suggested that we utilize the Washington office of Senator Strom Thurmond, then a Democrat, to find out what administrative remedies were available at Eisenhower's State Department.

Knowing that I was opposed to using political pressure in this matter, Travis was careful to assure me that none would be applied. We simply needed to know the rules by which the State Department operated on citizenship cases and Senator Thurmond's office could get the information quickly. So I authorized Travis to ask Thurmond to do us the favor.

I had met Strom Thurmond in 1956 on U.S. Highway 78 west of Augusta, Georgia. The Senator, who was driving his own Cadillac, explained that he seldom picked up hitchhikers, but decided to give me a ride because I had "an honest face." In answer to his questions, I told him my name and that I was going to Columbia, South Carolina, on the way back from Central America. He asked if they had segregation in Central America, and I replied that there was no legal separation of the races but that whites and Indians usually lived apart. Since Thurmond had no great interest in Latin America, our conversation soon turned to the United States Constitution. Before dropping me off on the highway to Columbia, the Senator took me to his brother's home in North Augusta, South Carolina, for Cokes and cookies. Thurmond was sincere and gracious, and although I disagreed with him on almost every question of the day, I couldn't help liking him.

Early in May 1960 Thurmond's assistant, Harry Dent, telephoned the State Department to inquire about the status of my case and the procedures for presenting evidence in defense of the accused. The Department replied in a letter to the Senator signed by Frances G. Knight, Director, Passport Office. Miss Knight's letters displayed the same arrogance—with only slightly more intelligence —as those of her fellow functionaries in Havana. She informed Thurmond that I had made an affidavit, supplementary to an application for registration as an American citizen in Cuba, which "stated that he went to Cuba to assist in the revolutionary movement, that soon after his arrival he joined the 26th of July revolutionary forces, and that he remained with these forces until his discharge from active service on his own request on March 23, 1959." She added that my case "was submitted to the Department for decision and the embassy at Habana was thereafter informed that in view of the information and evidence received it was considered that Mr. Macaulay had lost nationality . . . by serving in the Armed Forces of Cuba on and after January 2, 1959." Miss Knight didn't bother to mention that they were supposed to prove that I had served voluntarily after January 1, nor that none of her people had bothered to ask me about that. She did say that a certificate of loss of nationality was before her office for consideration, but that it had not yet been approved. She noted that "Mr. Dent has stated that an attorney acting in Mr. Macaulay's behalf wishes to present additional evidence for consideration. Accordingly, we will withhold action on the certificate of loss of nationality for a reasonable time in order to permit the submission of such evidence."

Since Miss Knight said she would allow us to present our side, Travis felt we had to go through the motions of submitting evidence to her office in order to strengthen our future case in the courts. Together we drew up an affidavit which I took to Gilchrist's office in Havana to be notarized. The balding Gilchrist looked the very stereotype of the harassed civil servant. Maybe he wasn't such a bad guy, I thought—but then I didn't offer him a copy of the affidavit. In the affidavit I explained the circumstances of my first statement: that I wasn't informed of the purpose for which it was to be used and, therefore, didn't bother to give the background of my discharge from Fidel's army. I noted my repeated attempts to resign, beginning on January 1, 1959, and declared that "at no time did I voluntarily serve in the Armed Forces of the Republic of Cuba."

It was arranged for Travis to present this affidavit to two lawyers from the State Department in Strom Thurmond's Washington office on July 5. At this meeting the men from the State Department admitted what Travis and I had long suspected: that they had no evidence other than my first affidavit and the two Rebel Army documents that I had allowed Miss Burnett to copy—none of which said anything about voluntary service after January 1. Senator Thurmond was present at the confrontation but, Travis assured me, exerted no pressure, though he did make one comment about having picked me up when I was "hitchhiking from Nicaragua and that he thought [I was] a nice fellow." One of the State Department lawyers replied, "Senator, we are going to decide this case on the evidence." Travis, impressed by the apparent fair-mindedness of his adversaries, recalculated the chances of the certificate being approved as fifty-fifty. He was satisfied that "we have met all administrative requirements and have laid a good groundwork for any other action that may be necessary."

When I learned that we had no cause for further action I was both disappointed and relieved. On July 13 Miss Knight wrote to Senator Thurmond that "in view of recent court decisions, particularly the Supreme Court decision in the case of *Nishikawa v. Dulles* which held that, regardless of what conduct is alleged to result in expatriation, whenever the issue of voluntariness is put in issue the Government must in each case prove voluntary conduct by clear, convincing, and unequivocal evidence, we have concluded that the Department could not sustain the burden of proof required to prove that Mr. Macaulay's service in the Armed Forces of Cuba on and after January 2, 1959 was, in fact, voluntary." Therefore, "the certificate of loss of United States nationality previously submitted by the American Embassy at Habana . . . is being disapproved and the Embassy is being authorized to accord him registration as a citizen of the United States." The registration was no longer appropriate; my wife and I had abandoned our Cuban residence the day before.

The business in Washington took much longer than we had anticipated. At the end of June we still hoped to be in Cuba when the State Department took its final action on the certificate of loss of nationality, but we went ahead and set our departure date for July 12 in order to accept the invitation of a friend, a member of the Ohio delegation to the Democratic Convention, to join him in Los Angeles. In the meantime, relations between Cuba and the United States took a dramatic turn for the worse: early in July President Eisenhower cut the Cuban sugar import quota and Fidel retaliated by nationalizing the American oil companies in Cuba. Nobody threatened my wife or me, but some ugly anti-American feeling was in the air and I was glad we were leaving. We kept our departure a secret from all our revolutionary friends.

On July 10 we traded cars. Che Guevara had decreed that no automobiles of Cuban registry, which included our 1959 Fiat, could be shipped from the island. We exchanged the Fiat for a 1952 Plymouth with Florida license plates that had been brought to Cuba on a thirty-day tourist visa by some missionary friends of the Willeys who planned to settle on the island. In a lawyer's office in Pinar del Río City we signed over our car to the missionaries and received a bill of sale for the Plymouth, a Florida registration card, a Cuban automobile visa, and the Havana–Key West portion of a round-trip ferry ticket.

The next day we organized our personal property—books, kitchenware, clothing, linens, crib, and playpen—for loading into the car after dark. By one of Che's decrees it was illegal to export electrical appliances, so we ripped out the innards of our largest suitcase and stuffed it with a coffee percolator, an iron, an electric frying pan, and a few other items; this we would carry to the airport, where the baggage of departing tourists wasn't normally searched. While the car was to go by ferry, my wife and I would take a plane to Key West, posing as an American couple with a year-old baby who were returning home after a brief visit to Cuba. I would drive the Plymouth to the ferry dock, embark it in the name of its former owner, and then take a bus to the airport to join my wife and the baby, whom Tommy Willey promised to transport there in his mission school bus.

The plan worked perfectly. We packed the car on the night of July 11, and I left for Havana before dawn. Tommy Willey came by the house a couple of hours later. I put the Plymouth on the ferry and met the rest of my family at the Aerovías Q airport shortly after they arrived. No officials at the airport recognized me or did anything to obstruct our departure. Early in the afternoon we were on a twin-engined plane airborne for Key West.

Among our fellow passengers were a number of middle-class Cubans on their way to exile. Their class valued freedom above all else, but never really understood that liberty cannot be won or maintained without discipline and self-sacrifice. In the United States they would enjoy the freedom that was denied them in Cuba and would be guaranteed a standard of living which, if lower than what they were accustomed to, was at least far superior to that of the Cuban peasantry before the Revolution. They were talented and industrious people who were capable of rebuilding their private fortunes in exile. But I doubted that they would ever recover what I knew to be their greatest loss: their country.

Index

195

Index

Index

Index

Index

A Note on the Author

Neill Macaulay was born in Columbia, South Carolina, and studied at The Citadel. He was graduated with General High Honors and served for two years as an officer in the United States Army, including duty in Korea. In 1958 he joined the Cuban Rebel Army of Fidel Castro in the Sierra de los Organos, Pinar del Río Province, Cuba. He served as a first lieutenant and staff officer, and later commanded a heavy-weapons platoon. He returned to the United States in 1960 to continue his education, receiving his M.A. from the University of South Carolina and his Ph.D. from the University of Texas. In 1965–1966 he did research in Brazil as a Ford Foundation Fellow, and he is now Associate Professor of History at the University of Florida. Mr. Macaulay is also the author of *The Sandino Affair*. He is married and the father of three sons.

N

Gulf of Mexico

Consolación del
Norte (La Palma)

La Mulata

Las
Pozas

Pan de
Guajaibón

S I E R

La Esperanza

San Vicente

San Diego
de los Baños

SI

Viñales

San Andrés

Los Palacios

Matahambre

SIERRA DE LOS ORGANOS

Consolación
del Sur

Pinar del Río

RÍO S. DIEGO DE LOS BAÑOS

Río Seco

Dayaniguas

Guane

San Juan y
Martínez

La Coloma

Gulf

Bay of
Cortez